PRAISE FOR GROW ORGANIC

"Want to go green? Co-authors Jessica Walliser and Doug Oster are terrific guides along the organic garden path. Learn how to feed your soil, befriend your bugs and bring in the bees, bolster your plants' immune systems, and support solutions rather than attacking problems. Safe, simple solutions are offered instead of toxic chemical fixes. If you've become an unwilling chore slave, you'll fall in love with your garden all over again as you learn to garden cooperatively with nature."

Ann Lovejoy
Author of *Ann Lovejoy's Organic Garden Design School,*
Gardening from Scratch, and many other titles

"Periodically a book about organic gardening comes along to call a new generation to responsible stewardship of the earth. Jess and Doug's friendly invitation to today's gardeners is encouraging and richly informative. Had I not been gardening organically for 25 years already, I would be inspired to run right outdoors and start!"

Liz Ball
Author of *Month by Month Gardening in Pennsylvania,*
Step-by-Step Yard Care, and many other titles

"A gentle, inspirational aid for homeowners looking to cut the chemicals from their outdoor life."

Mike McGrath
Host of NPR's "You Bet Your Garden,"
Former Editor-in-Chief, *Organic Gardening* magazine

"Walliser and Oster have put together the ideal guide to organic gardening... easy to follow, wide ranging, thorough and common sensical. This book tells it straight, making the principles easy to understand and follow. It's the ultimate guide to organic gardening!"

Chuck Leavell
Member of The Rolling Stones,
Author of *Forever Green: The History and Hope of the American Forest*

"*Grow Organic* proves once and for all that dousing your yard in toxic chemicals is so 20th Century. Beautiful, healthy, safe gardens work with nature, and Jessica and Doug take the mystery out of how to do it. This is practical, attainable advice delivered in a friendly, unthreatening way. Homeowners and gardeners both need this book."

Therese Ciesinski
Senior Editor, *Organic Gardening* magazine

"This is a great book filled with useful information – fun to read, straightforward and convincing. If you were not an organic gardener when you started, you will be by the end."

Holly H. Shimizu
Executive Director, United States Botanic Garden

"The jury is in: chemicals are out. Co-authors Jessica Walliser and Doug Oster 'tell all' with enthusiasm, wisdom and wit in *Grow Organic*. A treasure trove of tips presented in a conversational style, *Grow Organic* is a gentle but firm invitation for gardeners of all beliefs and backgrounds to embrace organic methods. A must-have manual for our busy world."

Marion Owen
Co-author of *The New York Times* bestseller,
Chicken Soup for the Gardener's Soul

"*Grow Organic* is a terrific primer for growers of any scale – in the backyard or in the back 40. With the need for a decentralized, ecologically sound system of food production becoming more critical with each passing year, and with the continued dilution of the term 'organic' in the marketplace, our hope is that the authors will inspire a whole new generation of truly organic growers."

Jodi & Evan Verbanic
Cherry Valley Organics

"All too often, our highly technologically driven lives separate us from the intricate environment we used to be so much a part of. We need to take a little time out to smell, listen and look at all that goes on around us. Gardening organically is such an effective way of putting us back in touch with our world; and *Grow Organic* will help us keep the world healthy and productive for our children and grandchildren."

Brent Heath
Author of *Tulips for American Gardens* and *Daffodils for North American Gardens*,
Owner of Brent and Becky's Bulbs

"*Grow Organic* makes gardening without chemicals possible for the average person. Its comprehensive yet accessible information provides everything you need to get started. Its easy-to-follow, conversational advice makes it feel like you're gardening with your best friend by your side."

Karen Keb Acevedo
Editor, *Hobby Farms* magazine

"Hats off to Jessica Walliser and Doug Oster for showing all of us how we can nurture the environment, one garden at a time. Enriched with personal anecdotes and a wealth of experience, *Grow Organic* is a perfect companion on your journey to a healthier, more satisfying gardening experience."

Jonathan Kaplan
Director, Sustainable Agriculture Project, Natural Resources Defense Council

"Jessica and Doug explain the art and science of organic gardening with clarity, passion and wit. Don't start another garden season without reading this book!"

Rob Cardillo
Garden Photographer; Author of *Totally Orchid*s and
The Complete Guide to Compost (as Robert Francis)

"It's ironic that many people who love to garden routinely apply pesticides and other unnatural chemicals – thereby potentially harming themselves, children, pets, birds, beneficial insects, earthworms, and everyone else on the planet. Oster and Walliser invite us to relearn the gardening secrets of our pre-DDT grandparents, and offer their own extensively researched and insightful ideas as well. But best of all is their enthusiasm – they'll convince you that you really can go organic, and do so triumphantly."

Debra Lee Baldwin
Author, *Designing with Succulents*

"We humans need to re-connect with nature. The authors do a great job of explaining how organic gardening can help us make that connection while providing safe, natural habitats for birds and other wildlife."

Timothy D. Schaeffer, Ph.D.
Pennsylvania State Director, National Audubon Society

"Doug and Jessica's weekly *Organic Gardening* show is one of our most loved radio programs. Their wealth of gardening knowledge coupled with their warmth and on-air charisma, generate extensive call-ins every week."

Rob Pratte
KDKA Radio, Pittsburgh

"*Grow Organic* is the perfect book for those interested in gardening naturally. It's about time that we had a publication like this! My wife and I planted our first garden together over 30 years ago and I wish we had this book then. Jess and Doug offer easy-to-understand advice on making responsible choices in the yard. Every home gardener, no matter the skill level, now has the ability to make a difference."

Brian Hill
President, The Pennsylvania Environmental Council

"For a retailer, the value of Jessica and Doug's knowledge about organic gardening is priceless. Their simple language, easy to understand tips and step-by-step methods make *Grow Organic* the perfect resource for all types of gardeners."

Randy Soergel
Owner, Soergel's Orchards

"Going organic is not just a personal health issue it is a commitment to caring about our global environment. Jessica and Doug make it easy to take the steps you need to succeed."

Richard Piacentini
Executive Director, Phipps Conservatory and Botanical Gardens

"Gardening organically is earth friendly and *Grow Organic* is reader friendly – abundantly full of tips that both new and long time gardeners can harvest. I will recommend *Grow Organic* to my customers seeking organic gardening info because it is easy to understand and so enjoyable to read."

Laurie Curl
Manager, Hahn Nursery

Grow Organic

GROW ORGANIC

DOUG OSTER AND JESSICA WALLISER

st. lynns press

PITTSBURGH

Grow Organic
Over 250 Tips and Ideas for Growing Flowers, Veggies, Lawns and More

ISBN-13: 978-0-9767631-6-1
ISBN-10: 0-9767631-6-8

Library of Congress Control Number: 2006939783
CIP information available upon request

First Edition, 2007

St. Lynn's Press • POB 18680 • Pittsburgh, PA 15236
412.466.0790 • www.stlynnspress.com

Cover Design – Jeff Nicoll
Book Design – Holly Wensel, NPS
Editor – Catherine Dees

Photo credits: Cover image copyright by Rob Cardillo; author photo copyright by Andy Starnes; photos on pages 49, 50 (top), 51, 52, 53, 54 (bottom), 124 (bottom) copyright by Doug Oster; photos on pages 50 (bottom), 54 (top), 55, 56, 121, 122, 123, 124 (top), 125, 126, 127, 128 copyright by Jessica Walliser.

Printed in the United States of America
on recycled paper

This title and all of St. Lynn's Press books may be purchased for educational, business, or sales promotional use.

For information please write:
Special Markets Department, St. Lynn's Press,
POB 18680, Pittsburgh, PA 15236

10 9 8 7 6 5 4 3 2 1

FOR CINDY

as every day passes I fall deeper in love with you

FOR JOHN AND TY

you fill every day with the best kind of sunshine

TABLE OF CONTENTS

To Our Readers

Our purpose in writing *Grow Organic* is to help you understand how truly satisfying organic growing can be. We want to de-mystify it for you, without softening the challenge or "dumbing" it down.

Do you dream of having a beautiful lawn, fruits and veggies to die for, a flower bed that just won't stop, and a garden environment where all of nature has the chance to thrive, including yourself? As fellow gardeners we can make this promise: it's all within your reach, whether you're just starting out or wanting to take an existing organic garden to the next level.

Inside this book are some unique features you aren't going to find in any other gardening book. We've dedicated an entire chapter to the transition process, showing you step by step how to make the switch to organic practices – on your own terms and within your own timeframe. There's a chapter on beneficial insects where you can read all about the connections between the "good bugs" in your garden and the health of your plants. Another chapter is dedicated to natural pest control and includes a simple 6-step plan to alleviate any pest woes you may encounter – an indispensable tool for all gardeners.

The life of a garden is ever-changing. Nature alters the garden, and so does the gardener, sometimes for the better and sometimes not. When we can learn from our own mistakes as well as the mistakes of other gardeners, it can be a real blessing. And so we have a **Tell-All** section in every chapter, where we share with you a special method or lesson we've each learned in our own gardens – "been there, done that."

In Chapters 2 through 9 you'll find sections called **Quick Tips**, where we put the practical information you need right at your fingertips. Quick Tips are the many practices and procedures that we both have found extremely helpful in our own gardens. For all you first-timers, no question is too elementary; we'll be here to explain every step and term. For you old-timers, our combined experience of nearly 50 years in the garden means we can offer **Advanced Quick Tips** as well – from soil prep to veggie perfection to unexpected ways to make your organic garden even better!

While much of *Grow Organic* is written for quick and easy reference, sometimes we like to dig a little deeper. Our **101** sections expand on single topics we think you'd like to know more about – like successful weed control or fail-proof composting. If you're attempting to resolve a particular issue in the garden, there's a handy **Index** in the back; also, a garden **Glossary** for explanations of unfamiliar terms.

Because we're organic gardeners ourselves, we know one of the most useful features will be the appendix titled **Friends of the Organic Gardener**. In it we give the names of companies and organizations we've come to rely on for valid, thorough information on organic gardening. You'll also find sources for many of the products we reference.

Throughout our book you will learn more about how your actions are connected to the life in your garden, and how you can act with purpose and thoughtfulness. Let *Grow Organic* be your guide to discovering how fulfilling it is to garden safely and organically. You and your family will be glad you did!

Doug Oster
Jessica Walliser

Organic Gardening
THE GUIDING PRINCIPLES

In farming, as in gardening, I happen to believe
that if you treat the land with love and respect,
then it will repay you in kind.

— Prince Charles

A garden should be a safe place – a place where children can run barefoot and robins are nourished by plump worms, and nobody has to worry about poisons. Poisons might seem like a strong word, but that's exactly what chemical pesticides and herbicides are. We know from experience that it can be hard to get information about gardening that doesn't involve the use of harmful chemicals; after all, the companies that produce alternative, healthy products for the garden don't have the multi-billion dollar marketing budgets that some of the big guys do. We feel that the best way to spread information about safe, responsible gardening is "over the fence" style, gardener to gardener.

That's exactly what we aim to do in the following pages: give you practical, effective information so you can make smart decisions in the garden and understand the challenges you are going to face (and the satisfactions). We want to arm you with all the know-how you'll need to garden organically. And we'll be with you every step of the way.

Why Go Green?

The term "organic" used in reference to gardening is relatively new. The concept, however, is not. Organic is how our great-grandparents gardened; they just didn't have a name for it. That was back before World War II, before we embarked on widespread research into the use of chemicals as weapons. Then came Vietnam and the defoliant Agent Orange, which evolved into 2,4-D, a common ingredient in today's weed-n-feeds. And before we realized what was happening, all kinds of other chemicals had crept into our gardens, masquerading as helpers. We have Rachel Carson to thank for telling us about the disastrous long-term effects of DDT (did you know, its inventor actually won the Nobel Prize for developing it?).

Before the 1940s, gardeners had no choice but to try to understand and connect with nature if they wanted a successful garden. They had no man-made, synthetic chemicals to reach for when there was a problem. They used nature's arsenal instead. In many ways, our great-grandparents had a better understanding of healthy soil and plants than we do. We've come to rely so much on the quick fix that we've lost sight of our own ability to garden in harmony with Mother Nature, instead of fighting her (and usually losing!). We need to reconnect with our gardening roots and get back to growing the way our ancestors did – organically.

Organic growing is practical in so many ways. Not only will it reduce your personal exposure to potentially toxic substances, but once your garden has made the transition to organic care (we'll learn about this in Chapter 2), you'll find it's easier on the budget too.

Some of the alternative products available may be more expensive than their conventional counterparts, but you'll be needing less and less of them with each passing season. Organic gardens that are properly managed don't need much intervention from us. The trick is learning when it's better to leave them alone.

Lots of folks want to garden more naturally, but aren't sure how. They wonder if they have the time or resources to make a complete conversion. We're here to say that even a small step in the direction of non-chemical gardening can make a huge difference in your life. We don't want to scare you (well, maybe we do), but if you don't already know the downside of a chemical-centered lifestyle, check out the following information:

1. Kids who grow up around conventional lawn and garden chemicals are 6 1/2 times more likely to get leukemia than kids who grow up in an untreated environment.

2. Dogs who romp on treated lawns are twice as likely to develop lymphoma.

3. Suburban lawns and gardens use more chemicals per acre than any other lands, including agricultural.

4. In the U.S., 67 million pounds of chemicals are applied to residential lawns each year.

5. Of the 36 most commonly used lawn pesticides: 14 are probable carcinogens, 15 are linked with birth defects, 21 are tied to reproductive disorders, 24 with neurotoxicity, 22 with liver or kidney damage, and 34 are classified as irritants.

6. The effects of exposure to pesticides can be both acute and chronic, and can range from headache and dizziness to heart attacks and cancer. Legally, manufacturers must provide a Material Safety Data Sheet to anyone who asks. Many are now available online and have startling data about these chemicals.

7. So-called "inert" ingredients in many pesticides are actually *more* harmful than the active ingredients and are unregulated and untested by the EPA. These secret ingredients make up over 95% of three quarters of the pesticides on the market today. Fifty of these ingredients are classified as highly toxic with known carcinogenicity, adverse reproductive health, and neurotoxicity.

8. The World Health Organization estimates that more than 200,000 people are killed by pesticide poisons worldwide, every year. This translates to 547 men, women and children dying every day from pesticide poisoning.

9. In studies done by the U.S. Department of Agriculture, 108 different kinds of pesticides were found on 22 fruits and vegetables. Sixteen pesticides were found in 8 samples of processed baby food.

These are scary facts, and there are lots more where they came from. We can blame agriculture and industry all we want for polluting our waters and fouling our air, but in reality, we are just as guilty as they are. Why do we continue to sacrifice our health and wellbeing to have a pest-free lawn and garden – especially when there are safe, affordable and effective alternatives? There was a time when we didn't understand what else these chemicals could do to us (and we were sold on their convenience). But now we do know, and we can change those statistics, starting with a few simple choices in the garden and around the house. There will never be a better time than right now for seeing what organic gardening is all about.

So You Want to be an Organic Gardener

Organic gardeners are thoughtful people. We not only care about our own health, but that of the soil, the native flora and fauna, our children, our neighbors. What makes someone an organic gardener? There's a long list of qualities; some are ideals, some are techniques and some are basic thought processes. An organic gardener is someone who:

- Understands their garden's connection with nature
- Cares for the soil by using only organic, earth-based materials
- Uses plant care products based solely on naturally occurring substances
- Eliminates the use of all synthetic herbicides and pesticides, all chemical fertilizers
- Promotes and encourages beneficial insects in the garden
- Understands the need to conserve resources in the garden and uses them wisely and only when necessary
- Nourishes their plants through the use of soil-building organic matter and naturally occurring mineral nutrients
- Mulches to cut down on watering and weeding
- Chooses naturally disease- and pest-resistant varieties suitable to their garden zone

- Tries to handle pest issues through the use of mechanical and preventive methods long before reaching for the spray bottle
- Understands that the goal is never to eliminate a pest from the garden, but to keep its population at tolerable levels
- Solves problems by taking the time to understand the issue through research and inquiry before taking action
- Educates others on the importance of natural care gardening
- Is healthier in both mind and body

Ambitious list, isn't it? Maybe at this moment you can only check off one or two items; maybe two years from now you'll be able to check off another two; or maybe you are so new to this that you don't even know what some of them mean. That's OK, everyone needs to start somewhere. We know that change can be difficult and we don't expect it to happen overnight. This list is simply a guide to help you understand and appreciate where this book is leading you. Every single modification you make will be for the better. We figure the more folks we can encourage to change even one little thing, the better off we all are. And we know there's safety in numbers!

Over the next eight chapters, each of these guidelines will become clearer and more realistic. The information for a complete conversion to organic care is all here – the rest is up to you.

So let's get diggin'...

Doug Tells All | *about going organic*

Many gardeners have an epiphany that starts them down the organic path. Mine happened after work one summer afternoon. I was new to gardening and relied mainly on the advice of conventional gardeners. When I started to see green caterpillars on my cabbage, I did what many novices do – I panicked. I called my friends and was told to dust the plants with Sevin. So I went down to the hardware store, bought a bag of the insecticide and covered the plants with the powder.

I stood triumphant as I looked over the garden – the conquering hero who had destroyed the invading force so determined to annihilate my crop. As I was smugly congratulating myself, my three-year-old son started to walk down the center path of the garden in search of some snow peas to pick off the vine. My smugness turned to dread in the pit of my stomach, and I thought, "What have I done?" That was my awakening, the innocence of a little boy searching for a fresh treat.

It was the last day I ever used chemicals in the garden, and my first as an organic gardener. I reveled in the fact that I was going to learn how to grow without pesticides and herbicides and finally take control of my own garden. It has been a wonderful journey of discovery and it's not over yet!

Jess Tells All | *about the little things*

When I graduated from a chemical-based college education (I have a degree in Ornamental Horticulture), I thought the only way to successfully grow plants was to nuke every pest and dump on the fertilizers. That's what I was taught and that's how I thought it had to be. A few years later, I made a friend who grew organically and another who was going through treatments for her infertility. Together they pointed out some of the pitfalls of those chemicals I was so wedded to. And that was it for me: I saw the light and I made the change. I know for others it may not be such an about-face. It may be a gradual realization and it may even be a challenge.

Whichever it is, I want you to know that there is no particular trick to becoming an organic gardener. There is no special club to join, no written-in-stone commitment you have to make to call yourself an organic gardener. Sure, I'd like you to be able to call yourself a 100% organic convert three hours after you finish reading this book, but I doubt that's going to happen.

With all of life, it's the little things that matter. Here are a few small things you can do that will help guide your thoughts in an "organic direction."

· *Subscribe to a magazine that specializes in organic gardening techniques.*

· *Get your feet wet by switching your houseplants to organic care.*

· *Buy only organically produced seed (we've got sources listed in the appendix).*

· *Grow a few veggies in your mixed perennial border (you'll tend to use less pesticide where food is growing).*

· *Read* The Botany of Desire: A Plant's-Eye View of the World, *by Michael Pollan.*

· *Purchase only plants that are naturally pest-resistant varieties.*

· *Run through the sprinkler at least once a week and hug your kids at least once a day.*

2

TAKING THE LEAP
YOUR GARDEN'S TRANSITION TO ORGANIC CARE

We have descended into the garden and caught three
hundred slugs. How I love the mixture of the beautiful
and the squalid in gardening. It makes it so lifelike.
— EVELYN UNDERHILL

The process of converting your garden to natural care is not necessarily quick and painless, especially for your plants. They may have been pumped with "steroids" of chemical fertilizers and surrounded by a force field of synthetic pesticides for years. In this chapter we'll explain what the changeover entails and why it's important to be patient and see it through.

Going Green Because You Care

You may expect your garden to bow down and thank you for switching to organic techniques. After all, now you're using "earth friendly" products. But, like a recovering addict, your garden will need time and understanding; and *you'll* need patience. On average, it takes two full years for your garden to adjust to a complete organic care conversion. Your soil will have to be rebuilt and your plants will have to learn to raise their own natural defenses. This doesn't mean, however, that you can't switch to organic care today – what it does mean is that your garden will need time to mend. The key to easing this period is your own understanding of the transition and its potential challenges. Knowing what to expect simplifies the entire process by leaps and bounds.

When you begin the conversion, you and your garden will go through several changes. Over the years, we have helped many gardens and gardeners transfer to organic care, so we are familiar with all these phases. In fact, we've discovered they are quite predictable.

In the beginning – You may notice an increase in pests when you stop using the manmade chemicals. Not everyone experiences this, but be aware that it may happen to you while you learn to control the bad guys organically. Your aim should be to keep their numbers manageable. In organic gardening, complete elimination of any pest is never the goal, and as a result you may need to increase your pest tolerance. In Chapter 9 we focus on natural pest management strategies and we really delve into the methods necessary to control these critters without harming the rest of the garden. The important thing to remember about this phase of the transition is that it is just that – a phase. Once you have completed the conversion process we detail below, your soil will be healthy, your plants vigorous and your garden in balance; and there will be a natural decrease in the pest population.

You'll find yourself referring to Chapter 9 a lot during the first year, and then less and less with each passing season. We promise that by the beginning of the second year (often sooner), you'll have a handle on the situation.

Getting into the game – As you start to wean your plants from their chemical dependency there is going to be a change in you. When you see holes in your Hosta leaves and pockmarks on your oregano you aren't going to like it; but instead of automatically reaching for a spray bottle you will begin to research solutions to the problem. Trust us, your plants are not going to die as a result of this damage (in this case, it's only aesthetic). Plants are patient; they will wait for you to get up and running. Some gardeners relish this learning process, others start to feel anxious. We encourage you to see it through (we even offer a Quick Tip about how to dispose of those toxic chemicals so you won't be tempted to use them!). Remember, this is all part of your garden's healing process.

Signs of Life – Within the first season of organic care you'll also begin to see an explosion of soil life – this is a very good thing! These soil-dwelling organisms – microbes, fungi and earthworms, to name just a few – are critical to your garden's overall health. Before the conversion, they were struggling to survive under the onslaught of chemicals. Even though you won't be able to see some of these microscopic creatures, their populations will continue to increase with every organic strategy you employ. And you'll appreciate the swell of the earthworm population every time you dig in your garden.

On the learning curve – The next phase you'll enter is a knowledge explosion. After you begin to see that these time-honored techniques are actually working (and easy!), you'll want to learn more. It will become a pleasant diversion to research a pest's life cycle or to decide which soil amendment is the best choice. Organic gardeners are always on the prowl for new methods and information about their plants. Perhaps you'll begin to take classes at a local organic farm or botanical garden; or maybe you'll find yourself volunteering in a community produce garden. Be willing to learn from others and don't hesitate to share your newfound knowledge of organic practices.

We've also discovered over the years that these phases will all occur no matter how much of the garden you are converting at any one time. Some of you may choose to switch your entire garden to organic management in one season – a sort of "cold turkey" approach. That's terrific, and we highly recommend it: it's less time consuming in the long run, but may be more nerve-racking, and requires a bit more study and diligence on your part. Many of you will likely choose a more gradual approach. That way you can get a feel for what's involved without being overwhelmed – it's a perfectly acceptable strategy. We want you to be successful no matter which plan you choose. The important thing is to create a transition plan for your garden and stick to it.

A gradual conversion plan – It can basically follow one of two paths. The first involves making a list of all the different areas of your garden that you plan to eventually convert; and then you prioritize them. Decide which areas are most important for you to convert to organic, and which can wait. Then you begin with one particular area of your property, say the lawn or the vegetable garden. Each year you continue down your list, converting each garden area separately. We recommend spending a full season switching each individual area.

Or...

You can start transferring the care of your entire garden to organic, but you'll employ one new organic practice at a time, over time. For example, this season you'll stop using chemical fertilizers while learning about proper soil management (Chapter 3), and then next year you'll begin using preventive pest deterrents instead of chemical sprays (Chapter 9). Depending on how determined you are to make the change, this method can take three or more seasons for a complete conversion.

Getting started with the transition is the hardest part for many gardeners. Let's talk about that next.

Just Do It! – an easy beginning

Whether you decide to use the "cold turkey" approach or one of the two gradual methods described above, some basic procedures will help ensure your success. Below, we have outlined a series of steps that walk you through the transition. Many of these steps are covered in far greater detail in future chapters of the book (we reference these chapters below). The progression we've chosen is very important; it will enable you to proceed without worry. As you read through the steps (and the entire book), it will become clear to you why we think this sequence works best.

Step 1:

We tell folks to begin the switch from the ground up – literally. Caring for your soil organically should be your initial undertaking. Many people think that eliminating pesticides in the garden is the first step in organic growing; to us this is putting the cart before the horse. We feel that starting with proper soil management will enable a natural reduction in the need for chemical pesticides in the garden by creating healthier, more vigorous plants. In Chapter 3 we explain all the essentials of healthy soil and how to use it to your advantage.

Step 2:

At this point it becomes important to focus your attention on understanding how to raise your plants' natural defenses to enable them to take care of themselves. In human beings, your immune system works better when you feed your body nutritious foods, exercise regularly and maintain a positive attitude. Plants have a primitive immune system too, and they respond to a malnourished immune system with decreased growth and vigor. There will also be increased susceptibility to pests and a greater propensity for disease. Insects can sense when a plant is vulnerable and will prey upon those specimens that are the feeblest, so it's important that we provide our plants with the right conditions for optimal growth. This is accomplished in the organic garden by building the soil, fostering beneficial insects (Chapter 4), feeding plants a healthy diet, not chemical junk food, and maintaining good cultural practices (see Step 4 below). After only a few months, you'll begin to see a real change in your plants. They will not suffer as much from insect attacks and they won't need so much attention from you.

Step 3:

Learn to love your bugs – the good and the bad. They are supposed to be there, and in the grand scheme of things they all have a purpose (although it's sometimes hard to see when a hornworm has just polished off an entire young tomato plant!). Appreciating all the life in your garden will help raise your pest tolerance. The vast majority (90%) of plant deaths are the gardener's fault, not Mother Nature's: the plant was planted, placed, fertilized, or cared for improperly and so it became susceptible to a pest and bit the dust.

Raising your pest tolerance is often the biggest challenge for new organic gardeners who aren't yet confident that they have done an effective job boosting their plants' natural defenses. For seasoned organic growers, the knowledge that a healthy plant can fight off an attack allows for a more relaxed approach to pests in the garden. This doesn't mean, however, that organic gardeners let munching insects take over the garden. What it does mean is that you'll eventually learn when it's the right time to step in and how best to respond.

Step 4:

Care for your garden appropriately. Good cultural practices prevent so many troubles in the garden. These practices include things like pruning properly, learning the best methods of staking and trellising plants, keeping the garden free of debris, not working in a wet garden, and mowing your grass to the correct height, to name just a few. We discuss cultural practices in each specific area of the garden throughout the book.

Step 5:

Pay attention to Mother Nature. As you convert your garden, she'll begin to cue you in on her own natural processes and you'll begin to use them to your advantage. Often, pest problems occur around the same time each season. If you note when the trouble generally starts, you can prevent the same malady from repeating itself next season. Pest crises may also occur under particular conditions – especially issues with disease and fungus. Any repeat of those conditions will warn you of potential problems before they arise, allowing you to use preventive measures for effective control. Mother Nature is a real ally in the organic garden; she always provides clues to our garden's needs. It's up to us to learn how to interpret them.

Step 6:

Now it's time to eliminate synthetic chemicals in the garden. Chapter 9 will guide you to a safer, non-toxic garden.

Patience is a Virtue

Every decision made in your garden needs to be a responsible and thoughtful one. For every move you make, nature will have a response. This is evident in the increasing amount of pesticide resistance now found in common garden pests. But, it's also true that an increase in organic-based care choices will result in nature providing you with more resilient and healthy plants. In organic gardening, the goal is to use only natural techniques to tend your plot. No matter how you get started, each step should be toward that end. Whether you are starting full force, following every bit of our advice, or just interested in changing one thing at a time, allow yourself time to learn. You'll receive a lot of counsel from other gardeners, some of it useful and some of it not. Decide which suggestions are right for you, and soon enough *you'll* be the one that others are turning to for guidance.

The final task in your organic transition is to have realistic expectations. The knowledge that nothing in your garden is going to be perfect is invaluable – a priceless truth for all gardeners to embrace.

Doug Tells All | *about the switch*

My initial decision to never again use chemicals in the garden was accompanied by a lot of fear. I thought every pest would converge on my garden, unleashing an onslaught of biblical proportions. Luckily, that never happened and my transition to organic growing was easier than I expected. Since I've never had to deal with diseases (thank goodness!), my only real concerns were potential pest troubles and improving my soil.

With only a rudimentary understanding of organics I started by handpicking most of the pests and I ended up with the most productive garden I'd ever had. As for the soil: each season my town gives away compost made from their collected fall leaves, so I began my first spring by bringing a few truckloads into the garden. I used it in my planting holes, for mulch and I even managed to save a little for future projects. I took the time to read everything I could about organic gardening and I fully embraced my new passion.

Later, when my gardening friends saw the end result of my transition, they wanted to know my secret. They began asking me questions, and my life changed forever. Not only was I officially an organic gardener, but now I was telling anyone who would listen about the joys, benefits and simplicity of gardening without chemicals. That was over 20 years ago and thankfully, people are still listening!

Jess Tells All — *about a whole new ballgame*

Imagine having to convince your boss to go organic; it's hard enough trying to sway family and friends! Years ago I began to tend nearly 30 perennial gardens around the city of Pittsburgh and many of them depended on chemicals. When I made the decision to convert to organic practices in my own home garden, I did it because I wanted to reduce my exposure to harmful substances. But just as important, I wanted to leave the Earth a better place than I found it. How could I go to work every day, spraying willy-nilly and not feel like I was failing myself?

I decided to simply tell my clients that I was no longer spraying any chemicals. I explained my position and passion for organics in an effort to convince them that these practices could work for them too. This was a tougher challenge than I expected. Undergoing the conversion in a single garden is one thing, but doing it in several gardens at the same time is a whole different ballgame.

The biggest issue, of course, was assuring my clients that they and their gardens would indeed survive. I knew that their confidence in organic practices would build with each success and, in the end, we would all be better off. Realizing the importance of education, both for myself and my clients, I spent long hours researching organic growing. I needed some information to back me up. I soon discovered that nothing encourages someone to try an organic method faster than quoting a university study proving its success!

QUICK TIPS

❧ COMMUNICATION ❧

If you can't say anything nice...

Sometimes the hardest part about seeing the transition through is the comments you'll receive from other gardeners. Visitors may point out pest problems and damaged plants and proceed to tell you what to do about it. Neighbors will remark about the big pile of compost on the driveway or how there are no dandelions in *their* yards. Instead of feeling embarrassed by these temporary issues, use the opportunity to inform them about the importance of organic techniques for the community as a whole.

Dandelions

Explain to your neighbors how nutritious and delicious dandelions can be! Tell them that in Europe they are hybridizing them as garden specimens to grow in perennial borders; they are not weeds, they are native wildflowers.

A family affair

Talk to your family about your conversion. Tell them about some of the changes that will be taking place and why it's important for everyone to be onboard. We can't tell you how many times people have told us that they want to convert to organic practices but their loved one won't stop using the lawn company. It's important that you express your feelings about chemical-based gardening and tell your family why they need to be patient during the transition.

❧ KIDS IN THE GARDEN ❧

Kids and bugs

Get kids involved during this transition period. There has never been a safer time for them to romp in the garden. Arm them with a bucket of soapy water and set them to work picking off Japanese beetles and cabbage loopers.

Kids and plants

Give your children a corner of the garden to try growing their own vegetables and flowers. Let them choose the design of their patch and what plants they'll grow. No one wants to use toxic chemicals around their children. And in the process, you may very well make a gardener for life!

Kids and seeds

The bigger the seed the better for children. Beans are the perfect size for little hands. Have patience when they plant 10 seeds in the same place; that's part of the learning process.

Kids and your commitment

Nothing will keep you from reaching for a spray bottle better than the conscience of a child. Tell your kids the dangers of synthetic garden chemicals and explain to them why you are switching to organic practices. Trust us, every time you spray something in the garden they will ask you what it is and why you are using it. And they will be sure to remind you repeatedly about the commitment you've made.

Kids and weeds

Kids love to earn a few extra bucks. In our day we made a penny apiece for each dandelion flower we picked. Calculate the increase in the cost of living and it might be 5 cents now (depending on the age of the kid). Take a quick look at the lawn before you make the offer; your industrious little one might just break the bank.

❧ SAVVY CATALOGS ❧

Using catalogs as a resource

Request catalogs from as many organic product suppliers as you can. Many of these publications are not just selling you products, they are providing you with information. Even if you never buy, use them as a resource. Some catalogs have well-photographed pest identification keys, while others contain charts and graphs of things like planting times and fertilizer preferences.

✎ A NEW APPRECIATION ✎

Tooling up

Invest in some new garden tools. Nothing says "I'm turning over a new leaf" like a good, sharp pair of pruners or a shiny new pitchfork.

Appreciating the garden

Take time to sit in the garden and watch the wildlife. Birds, bees, ants, chipmunks, toads, spiders and butterflies are all amazing creatures. Do the same thing at night. Watch the fireflies, moths, bats and, yes, even the slugs.

The barefoot gardener

Work with naked feet. The feel of the soil between your toes and the grass tickling your tootsies will remind you of simpler times.

✎ PREVENTION IS THE KEY ✎

Mildew prevention

Mix 1 tablespoon of baking soda and 1 teaspoon of mild dish soap with a half-gallon of water to make an organic fungicide that will help prevent black spot and powdery mildew. Begin to spray early in the season and continue every 2 or 3 weeks.

Blight prevention

Give tomatoes plenty of room to grow. Spacing them about 3 feet apart will go a long way toward preventing fungal diseases. Mulching them will also prevent soil-borne diseases from splashing up onto the leaves.

Vine borer prevention

To prevent squash vine borers from attacking the base of your zucchini and squash plants, cut a strip of aluminum foil about 2" x 6" and wrap it loosely around the stem. Do this as close to the soil as possible and the adult insect won't land there to lay its eggs.

Fungus prevention

Watering your garden early in the day will prevent many fungal issues. Since these diseases thrive on wet foliage, time your watering so the plants will have ample time to dry before nightfall.

Smart plant picks

One of the easiest ways to reduce the amount of chemicals needed in your garden is to choose pest-resistant varieties. When shopping for new plants, do a little research. Find out which choices aren't prone to diseases like powdery mildew or bacterial wilt. Ask gardening friends which plants are most resilient in their gardens.

Invasion

One way to simplify your life in the garden is to pay attention to the potential invasiveness of any plants you are introducing. If a catalog touts a plant as quick spreading, watch out. Some species can quickly outgrow their desired location and crowd out more desirable plants. Your county's cooperative extension agency can also provide you with a list of invasive species in your area.

Tried and true

Simplify your garden during the transition period by planting it with old standbys. Lots of traditional garden plants are still being grown simply for the fact that they aren't prone to pest and diseases. Skip the fancy, untried varieties for a season or two and go with marigolds and Cosmos.

Or go native!

Try growing native plants. They are tough, pest-resistant and used to growing in your climate.

Wildflowers

If there's a section of the garden that you'd like to transition to organic care, but you aren't quite ready to go full-force, sow some annual wildflowers. Choose a native mix that will easily fill the space with care-free, easy to maintain flowers. When you are ready for the full transition, till them under or plant between them. Wildflowers will keep any bare ground from eroding and help bolster the population of beneficial insects (see Chapter 4 for more info about beneficials).

Weeds

If weeds are the pest you are looking to prevent, try corn gluten meal. It's a by-product of the processing of corn and acts as a pre-emergent herbicide: it prevents seeds from sprouting. Use it on the lawn and in the perennial border. Just be sure not to use it where you'll be growing plants from seed. With regular use, it can prevent 90% of weed seeds from germinating. Imagine, 90% fewer weeds to pull!

More about weeds

Leave a corner of the garden wild. It's a place that will attract lots of beneficial insects and produce seeds for the birds.

ADVANCED QUICK TIPS

(Longtime organic gardeners have already gone through the transition process, so this chapter's Advanced Quick Tips offers a few reminders and maybe a new idea or two.)

❧ REMINDERS ❧

Free plants!

Do some drive-by's of your favorite neighborhood gardens. Check out which plants seem to be the most resilient and be sure to compliment the resident gardener. Then ask them for a plant ID – this may just lead to an offer to share a division with you.

Plant swaps

A nice way to make new gardening friends, and obtain some new plant material, is to host a plant swap. Invite every gardener you know, from novice to expert, and ask them to each bring 5 labeled plants. They can be divisions from their own gardens or seeds they have started indoors. Have some reference books handy for folks to investigate any unfamiliar plants, then cut your guests loose. Everyone leaves with the same number of plants they brought, plus a few new gardening pals.

A little dirt never hurt anyone

Most gardeners love to get dirt under their fingernails, but if you're not fond of it, scratch a bar of soap before starting to work in the garden. When you are done, the soap will wash out from under the nails, taking the dirt with it.

Water

Make sure your plants are never left high and dry. Most garden plants need 1 inch of water per week to thrive. If you let your plants get too dry, they will suffer from "water stress." The biggest symptom, of course, is wilting; but regularly subjecting your plants to this stress will reduce their natural immunity, causing them to be more susceptible to problems.

Disposing of chemicals

Eliminate chemicals in the garden by disposing of the ones you've already got and vowing to never purchase more. You can learn how to properly rid your garage or garden shed of these chemicals by contacting your municipal or county office and asking when they will be holding a hazardous waste collection.

✄ BOOSTING THOSE DEFENSES ✄

Liquid compost and disease suppression

Compost tea is terrific for boosting a plant's natural defenses. Brew some up by steeping a few shovelfuls of compost (wrapped in burlap) in a bin of water. Use this concoction to water your plants. And be sure to get the foliage wet too; recent studies have shown that compost tea protects the leaves from soil-borne diseases and blights.

✄ EXAMINING YOURSELF...AND NATURE ✄

Journaling

Every stage of your garden's evolution is a learning experience. If you haven't already, start a garden journal and record everything you observe in the garden, from butterflies to slugs. Use it as a place to document names of new plants, phone numbers of mulch suppliers, and sketches of unidentifiable insects. Write down how you are feeling each time you dig into your soil, and make plans for future garden projects.

Up close and personal

Buy a small hand lens or magnifying glass to examine garden pests at work. Sometimes we don't appreciate nature until we take a good, hard look at her intricacies. The lacy wings of an aphid or the white fuzz on a mealy bug may not seem like works of art, but under closer inspection they are beautiful in their own way. (Of course, it's even cooler to watch a ladybug devour that aphid!)

3

THE REAL DIRT
ORGANIC SOIL MANAGEMENT

*Opportunity is missed by most people
because it is dressed in overalls and looks like work.*
— THOMAS A. EDISON

The foundation of your organic garden is your soil. By understanding and improving your soil, you can virtually guarantee a successful organic garden. In this chapter we will give you the simple essentials of soil composition and soil management.

The Lowdown on Your Soil's Composition

We're going to let you in on a little secret: the color of your thumb has little to do with your prowess in the garden. What really makes or breaks your horticultural abilities is right there beneath your big size 9s. Yep, that's right, your soil. We know that paying attention to the soil is not the most glamorous job in the garden, but it is the most essential. Caring for your soil means looking at what it's actually made of, and then figuring out how we can improve upon what nature handed us. More often than not, it also means lugging wheelbarrows and wheelbarrows full of organic matter; and thinking about stuff like earthworms, microbes, science and chemistry (don't worry about the science and chemistry part – we'll help you with that too).

Your garden really does start with your soil – especially your organic garden. When you think about it, you can compare your garden's soil with your own body. The earth cannot live by chemical fertilizers alone, just as you can't survive on just a daily vitamin. We need more than that to thrive, and so do our plants.

Understanding your soil's composition is the first step in this process. So what's in the average sample of garden soil? From a teaspoon to a truckload, all soil samples have essentially the same basic ingredients, just in different proportions.

Let's look at the mineral components of your dirt. These come from rocks that have broken down over millions of years and are grouped into three categories:

- sand
- silt
- clay

The biggest pieces are sand, which we can see with the naked eye. They feel gritty and are well drained. In the middle of the group are the silt particles, feeling slippery when wet and powdery when dry. The littlest pieces, the clays, are flat and stack on top of each other like sheets of paper. Clay is sticky when wet and very poorly drained. The percentage of each of these three particles in any given soil determines its *texture*.

The U.S. Department of Agriculture has a fancy pyramid that they use to determine which texture class your soil fits into. Without needing to spend a lot of money to have a classification test done, you can get a basic understanding of your soil's texture by just examining it. If your soil is clay-based, you can see it stick to the bottom of your boots when you walk through the garden after a rain. In the case of a sandy soil, you can feel its gritty, grainy consistency every time you plant.

It's good to know what you've got, but the truth is, no matter how hard you try, you can't change your soil's texture. A sandy soil will always be a sandy soil, and the same for clay – so don't think that adding sand to your clay soil is going to make it any better. Instead, focus on your soil's *structure*.

The Digs on Dirt: soil structure and health

Good soil structure is what creates that black, crumbly soil we see on all those gardening TV shows. Structure refers to the way the sand, silt and clay particles stick together or aggregate. If you're lucky, your soil already makes those nice little, crumbly clumps; if you're not lucky (and, really, who is?) it either falls apart in your hands and runs through your fingers, or sits in one massive hard lump at the end of your shovel. How these particles stick together is so important because it determines how the water, air, and nutrients move around in your soil. If you don't have nice crumbles, your soil may stay waterlogged well into the spring or it may drain too quickly, leaving your plants very thirsty even after a rain.

The secret to getting those TV crumbles is *organic matter*. Only 1 to 6 % of that ideal soil sample is going to be organic matter – dead and decaying stuff – but, oh, how important that small dose is! It's the life of your soil; it's the bridge that binds; it's food for your plants; it's energy for the microbes; it's a moisture absorbing sponge; and it's the secret behind Martha Stewart's empire.

The road to good soil structure is always uphill, and there you are, standing at the bottom with that wheelbarrow. The more organic matter your soil has, the better your garden will be – and *you've* got to put it there.

In the following chart we've listed our favorite organic matter sources, with a little bit about each one. It's important to remember that you've got to maintain a balance in your soil, so choose your organic matter appropriately and mix it up each year. Don't apply the same thing year after year; variety is the spice of soil life!

Soil amendment	Average pH	Nutritional analysis	Our comments
Compost, either home-made or commercially produced.	7 (To learn about pH, go to page 30)	Compost is typically well balanced and contains a great blend of all nutrients.	Good quality compost should smell earthy and be rich, dark brown. Check with any commercial source to ensure that bio-solids (sludge) were not used. If the product smells like urine, it's likely the nitrogen content is too high. It's always best to make your own compost to ensure it is balanced and well rotted, though quality commercial composts do exist.
Mushroom soil or mushroom compost	8	Fairly high in organic matter. Low nutrient levels, but they are slowly released over time so they are constantly available.	A by-product of mushroom production, this compost contains ingredients like horse manure and shredded corn cobs. It can be fairly high in soluble salts but also contains a substantial amount of organic matter. Because of its high pH we don't recommend adding it every year.
Sphagnum peat moss	4	Very low in all nutrients.	Peat moss helps loosen compacted soils, but can alter the pH. It's weed-free but adds very few nutrients to the soil. Great choice for acid loving evergreens.
Leaf mold or leaf humus	7.5	Moderate but balanced nutrient levels. Also contains many minor nutrients.	Primarily composed of municipally collected leaves, these products are high in many trace nutrients as well. They've also got great water holding capacity.
Manures	Depends on type	Highly variable, but generally very high in all nutrients. Also depends on what materials were used in the animals' bedding.	All manures are not created equal. Horse and cow manures are more mild, while chicken and sheep are highly concentrated. Manures contain many weed seeds and should be composted for at least 90 days before use.

Healthy dirt has billions and billions of living organisms in it. From the smallest microbes and microscopic fungus and earthworms to big old ground-hogs – they all play an important role in your soil's health. They mix it, process it, and change the way it sticks together. Promoting substantial organic matter content encourages soil life to do its best job. Those critters are essential in releasing nutrients to your plants and greatly influence the overall vigor of your garden.

If at this time you can't add a lot of organic matter (maybe your back or your budget protest) you can substitute with some organic granular fertilizer. Keep in mind that this is still simply the vitamin; it is not the foundation your garden needs. Please see Chapter 6 for more information about fertilizer selection.

Compost 101 – Doug's way

Throughout the book you'll hear us sing the praises of compost – it's a great way to get rich, organic soil. Compost is something that you can create on your own with a little bit of effort, and it is one of the highest quality sources of organic matter. Here's the scoop on how to make your own "black gold" – the easy way.

Anything that once was living will eventually turn into compost; it's the result of insects, bacteria, fungus and earthworms devouring and processing the materials we provide them. If you want to make your own compost, follow these simple instructions:

My favorite system relies on **three bins**, each measuring 3'x3'x3' and placed in a row. Mine are made from used pallets nailed together, but you could use concrete block, recycled lumber or even hay bales. Bin #1 is the working pile; in it goes the fresh material (we'll talk about the fresh material below). As bin #1 fills and begins to age, turn the pile by transferring it into bin #2. Each time a bin is filled, its partially decomposed contents are just moved down the line. By the time the material is ready to move out of bin #3, it's finished and ready to spread.

If you don't have the space for a three-bin system, there is also a wide variety of commercial bins and compost tumblers on the market. Because turning your compost can make it decompose up to 50% faster (it introduces much needed air to the microbes), be sure to have your bin located somewhere that is easily accessible. There is also the "pile it up and wait" method, which happens to be Jess's favorite. This requires a bit of patience – it may take years for the material to break down, but it sure is easy.

The perfect compost pile has a 3:1 carbon to nitrogen ratio. This means that you'll want 3 times more dried, brown ingredients (carbon sources) than fresh, green material (nitrogen sources). This will keep your pile's moisture content just right and keep it decomposing at a good clip. Green materials include grass clippings, kitchen scraps (no meat, oils or dairy), weeds, fresh trimmings, manure (not from dogs or cats, please) and over-ripe veggies. Browns include hay, straw, autumn leaves, shredded newspaper, unbleached napkins and paper towels. I keep a few bags of leaves or a bale of hay right next to the pile, so as summer progresses and I have ample green materials, I can just throw in a few buckets of brown ingredients as I go.

There are two more ingredients needed to keep that pile cooking: moisture and oxygen. The oxygen is provided every time you turn your pile. You can also sink a perforated PVC pipe into the pile to get air to the lower layers. As for the moisture, form a slight depression in the top of the pile to collect rainwater. If you're using a closed bin, rinse the kitchen scrap bucket and add the water to the bin. You can also add water from the hose. The ideal moisture content should make your working pile feel like a wrung out sponge.

Of course, you can always buy bagged or bulk compost at your local nursery; but then you never know what you are getting. You might be spreading bio-solids or you might have just paid a pretty penny for a bag of pine bark nuggets labeled as compost. Making your own compost is a great way to recycle yard debris and create your own perfect fertilizer.

Doug

---

pH Perfection

If you know only one thing about your soil, know its pH. That is its most important property. The term "pH" is science talk for the measure of the acidity of your soil. It is so important because pH determines the availability of all the nutrients in your soil. If the number is too high or too low, it doesn't matter how much fertilizer or organic matter you throw on – your plants can't access the nutrients, which will remain tied up in the soil. The majority of garden plants, with the definite exception of evergreens, prefer a pH of about 6.5, or very slightly acidic (7 is neutral on the scale of 0-14). At pH 6.5 the greatest number of nutrients are available to a plant, no matter what the soil type.

Let's say you take a soil test (see the Friends of the Organic Gardener appendix for a list of soil test sources) and your pH isn't optimum. You'll have to do one of two things to correct it and you'll have to do these *before* you do anything else to your soil:

- If the number comes back too low (acidic), add the recommended amount of lime. We prefer Dolomitic limestone – it's a great source of both calcium and magnesium.

- If the number comes back too high (alkaline), add elemental sulfur.

Test your pH again in a few months to make sure the change took place and your pH is now correct. Nothing is more important than getting to the magic 6.5. Combining the magic number with lots of organic matter will result in your best garden ever.

Even Manure is Going Green – cover cropping

There's something else organic gardeners can do to raise their soil's organic matter content, and it doesn't even require a wheelbarrow. It's called cover cropping. Otherwise known as "green manure," cover crops are plants grown specifically for use in their afterlife. Typically planted at the end of a growing season, they are left to grow until the following spring and then turned into the soil before the new season's planting occurs. It's amazing how throwing a couple of seeds down in the fall can add a huge amount of nutrients to your soil for the following season.

Cover crops are selected based on what your soil needs. The most common choices are in the pea (or legume) family. Crops like alfalfa, hairy vetch, or cow peas are preferred because legumes have the unique ability to convert nitrogen from the air into a form that plants can use. When we till these plants into the soil each spring they slowly release their "fixed" nitrogen into the soil where it can be used by the current year's crops.

Keep in mind that cover cropping can really become an excellent soil management technique in even the smallest garden. By planting a cover crop and never leaving an area fallow you will prevent soil loss due to erosion; plus, the decomposition will add more organic matter and nutrients. We usually recommend mowing down cover crops before tilling the soil so they break down faster (not to mention that it makes it lots easier to turn the spade!). A list of our favorite cover crop seed sources can be found in the appendix. These companies will be able to help you select the proper cover crop for your growing needs and climate.

You can also plant cover crops between veggies, making a sort of living mulch. We love to see red clover underneath tomato plants, knowing that the clover is not only cutting down on watering and adding to next year's nutrients, but also attracting beneficial insects (more about those guys in Chapter 4.)

Mulch Matters

The term "mulch" refers to anything that is applied to the soil's surface with the following purposes in mind: controlling weeds, stabilizing soil temperatures, cutting down on watering, and beautification. That can include using gravel, plastic or shredded rubber – none of which adds organic matter to your garden and in fact can actually do harm (rubber may add heavy metals and plastic may "bake" the roots of shrubs or harm soil life). But many other kinds of mulch will enrich your soil and contribute organic matter.

This chart lists our favorite mulches, what they're good for and where it's appropriate to use them.

Mulch type	Where to use	Our comments
Compost, either home-made or commercially produced.	Use to mulch perennial, annual and shrub beds. Also good for the vegetable garden.	Compost makes great mulch. When fully composted there are very few weed seeds and it has a dark, rich appearance. One inch of compost will also supply all the nutrients your plants need for a full season's growth. It looks especially nice in the perennial border. Compost comes screened into different sizes – choose whichever one you like best.
Mushroom soil or mushroom compost	Typically used in perennial and annual areas.	Don't use alkaline mushroom soil to mulch the foundation beds of your house. These beds often contain evergreens which prefer acid soils. It is best applied only 1 to 2 inches deep and only once every 2 to 3 years to prevent any soil pH change.
Shredded bark	Use only around trees and shrubs.	Bark mulch is not fully decomposed, and as it continues to break down it robs small amounts of nitrogen from your soil. It's a great choice for shrub beds because it takes several years to break down, so you only need to mulch those areas every few years.
Straw or hay	This material is perfect for use on garden paths and in the vegetable garden.	Our favorite use of hay and straw is in the veggie garden under tomatoes, zucchini and others. It keeps soil from dirtying the produce and helps suppress soil-borne diseases. Straw and hay do contain weed seeds so we recommend using them on top of layers of newspaper or weed fabric when possible.
Grass clippings	Best used in the vegetable patch, between rows and on paths.	Make sure the clippings come only from lawns not treated with chemical pesticides or herbicides. Only apply about 1 inch thick to prevent a mat from forming. Once decomposed, they are a great nitrogen source for your plants.
Newspaper	Use in the vegetable garden or in areas where annuals will be densely planted.	Lay down about 10 sheets of newspaper and wet to keep them in place. Cut holes in the paper and plant. Cover the newspaper with straw, hay or any other attractive mulch. The papers can be tilled into the garden the following spring. Do not use the shiny inserts because they may contain heavy metals.
Cocoa hulls, rice hulls or buckwheat hulls	Mainly used in perennial and annual areas.	We aren't very fond of these because of their coarse nature and the fragrance of the cocoa hulls. They can be relatively expensive. On the plus side, they do take two seasons to fully decompose and some people actually like the smell of chocolate in their garden.
Shredded leaves	Use around perennials, trees, shrubs and veggies.	Finely chop your fall leaves before applying them as mulch. Never use whole leaves as they can form a mat and prevent water from reaching the soil. Any type of leaf is fine, but a mixture is best. You can run them over with the lawn mower or through a chipper/shredder before use.

You'll notice that several of these products were also mentioned in the soil amendment chart on page 28. Here's the difference: When you use the material as mulch it's only applied to the soil surface, while a soil amendment is mixed in with your existing soil. In either instance, the application of any of these materials is adding organic matter to your soil.

As with anything else in life, technique matters. We can't tell you how many times we've driven by houses with mulch piled up around trees or other plants in a big volcano. You're essentially forcing the plant's demise when you mulch improperly. The trick is to never let the mulch come in contact with the plant itself; be sure that it stays a few inches away from the base. By doing this you ensure that the heat of the decomposing mulch will not burn the plant, nor will excess water against the stem cause rot. It also keeps bark-chewing rodents at bay during the winter months. Mulching is imperative in the organic garden, and doing it with care will benefit both plant and soil.

Nurturing your soil will inevitably lead to a thriving organic garden, making your plants healthier, more resistant to pests, more tolerant of disease and more fruitful. Take good care of your little bit of earth, and it will take care of you.

Doug Tells All *about preparing the soil for spring planting*

"Successful gardening is doing what needs to be done, the way it needs to be done, when it needs to be done, whether you feel like doing it or not." There's a lot of truth behind that old saying. Like comedy, gardening is all about timing, and that's especially true early in the season. There's a window of opportunity when preparing your soil for spring planting. The window is only open for a couple of weeks after the snow melts; it closes when those April showers begin. If you put off your soil preparation there's a good chance you'll be facing weeks of monsoon rains that leave you staring out the kitchen window longingly. You'll wish you'd gotten up off that couch and started digging! Each spring, when the weather breaks, I get my tools sharpened and jump into action.

On the back of that packet of peas you'll read, "Plant as soon as the soil can be worked" – a frustrating statement for beginners who wonder exactly when that is. There's a simple test to determine if the soil is ready. Take a shovel out to the garden and turn it over in a couple of spots. If the soil sticks to the shovel, forget it and try again in a few days.

If you are lucky and the weather cooperates, your garden will be ready to go well before the last frost date. But even better, your beds will be ready for cool season crops like lettuce and pansies. It's a great feeling when planting time arrives and your soil is soft and ready to accept your treasured seedlings.

Jess Tells All *about planting a cover crop*

Gardening is filled with discoveries – that's why I love it. Each time we venture into the garden we learn something new, for better or worse. One of my latest revelations: Using cover crops isn't necessarily easy. A few years ago, I decided to get serious about this cover crop thing, so I purchased some field rye mixed with hairy vetch. I'd always read to simply distribute the seeds in the fall and turn them under in the spring, so that's what I did. Apparently there's more to it than that.

Here's what I learned:

First off, don't sow the seed too thick; you'll end up with a mat so dense that tilling is practically impossible (trust me, I know!).

Secondly, cut down the plants with a mulching mower right before you plan to till, otherwise they won't break down quickly enough. After turning them under, wait at least two weeks before planting. The soil takes time to settle and you'll want the decomposition process to start before you begin messing around in there.

And finally, there will be cover crop "babies" that pop up in the garden all season long. I'm still finding hairy vetch twining up my tomato cages.

Now I know to till cover crops under very carefully and to be a little more vigilant in my choice of varieties. I also understand that the benefits of using cover crops far outweigh any negatives. After only three years of using "green manure" I have absolutely beautiful, rich soil…ahhh, another lesson learned!

QUICK TIPS

✄ COMPOST ✄

Free municipal compost

Many municipalities offer free compost to residents. Usually made from leaves and other yard waste collected from parks and residences, it can be a nice addition to the garden. If you're concerned about its content, simply ask. The municipality should be able to share their material sources with you. Be warned though, anything brought into the garden can contain noxious weed seeds. Keep a close eye on the applied areas to see what sprouts – then take action immediately.

The sniff test

When buying commercially produced compost either in bags or bulk, ask to smell it. No reputable nursery will turn you down. It should smell earthy and musty, not acidic or sour. Always ask if the compost was made using sewage sludge – an ingredient, in our opinions, not considered safe for organic gardens.

Compost in your potting mix

Compost makes a great addition to potting mixes in containers. Ever plant your containers and slowly watch them dwindle in beauty throughout the year? Mix a shovel of compost with your light potting mix for a natural slow-release fertilizer. No need for those water soluble chemical fertilizers!

Sifting

Even finished compost will still contain some larger pieces. Use hardware cloth attached to a 2' x 4' frame to sift the compost before using it in the garden. Add the bigger pieces back into a working pile.

Wood ashes?

Be sure to compost your wood ashes before adding them to the garden. They can quickly alter the pH of your soil, so add them to the compost pile first.

To achieve the proper balance, be sure there's an ample amount of other products in your heap. Never use ashes from charcoal or coal in the garden. They contain chemicals that can adversely affect your plants.

✄ MULCH (WHERE, HOW AND WHEN) ✄

In established perennial beds

When attempting to add organic matter to your established perennial beds, don't try to work it into the soil. Instead use it as mulch. Simply adding 1 inch of compost as a top dressing will provide all the nutrients your perennials need for a full season's growth. Remember, never pile the organic matter onto the plant itself; keep it a few inches away from the crown.

Landscape fabric

Use black landscape fabric to get an early start on your planting. Lay it over the soil two weeks before planting time to help raise soil temperatures. Tomatoes, peppers and cukes prefer warm soil and can be planted right through holes cut in the fabric. Put a mulch of straw or hay on top.

Weed prevention

Keeping the soil free of weeds is a season-long challenge. Weeds rob your plants of nutrients and water. Mulch as soon as the spring soil warms, and remove weed seedlings upon emergence. Try to eliminate as many young weeds as possible before adding the mulch – don't just dump the mulch on top. Start the spring weed-less; it will make for a much easier summer!

✄ COVER CROP EXTRAS ✄

As edibles

Some cover crops have a dual purpose. Use beans, peas or soybeans as an edible cover crop. They fix nitrogen in the soil and then make a tasty treat at harvest time. Till them under at the end of the season.

As living mulch

Using cover crops as living mulch is an awesome labor saver. Plant red clover, alfalfa or another green manure right underneath your squash, pumpkins, peppers, tomatoes and cucumbers. No weeds will compete with the cover crop and you'll cut down on your watering by having less soil exposed to evaporation. You can also plant cover crops between your rows and periodically mow it throughout the season.

✖ WHEELBARROW, SPADE AND SHOVEL ✖

Easy does it

When moving a wheelbarrow over a curb, turn it around and pull it up and over; it's much easier on both your back and the tire.

Saving wear and tear on your soil

Lay 6-inch-wide boards down when you spread organic matter in the vegetable patch. Drive the wheelbarrow on the boards to prevent both soil compaction and a gunked up tire.

Tiller vs. shovel

If possible, use a shovel to turn the garden, not a tiller. Soil structure can be altered by excessive tilling. Digging the soil by hand is a great workout and a good way to examine the quality of soil in each bed.

Quick and easy edging

For impeccable garden edges, use a flat spade with a short handle. Turn the spade so the back of it is facing away from your body and tilt it so the handle is at your waist level. With quick stabbing motions, chop 1 inch of sod off the garden's edge and simply twist the handle of the shovel to flick it away. Collect the trimmed-off sod pieces and toss them into the compost pile. This is the quickest edging method we've ever seen! It looks great and will keep the grass out of your beds.

✂ SOIL ✂

Sampling

When taking a soil test, it's important to get a representative sample. Instead of removing soil from only one place in the garden, take many small samples and mix them in a bucket. Take your testing sample from this; you'll get a more accurate picture of the soil in the entire garden area.

Indoor dirt

Don't use garden soil for indoor plants. It's much too heavy, and it's often poor draining. You risk suffocating the roots and bringing in critters that should be kept outdoors. Houseplants and other potted specimens should be grown in light potting mixes.

Moles

Believe it or not, moles can be your friends. They don't feed on plant roots and their presence usually means one of two things: you've got a healthy earthworm population (great!) or a healthy grub population (not great). We recommend that you simply step down the tunnels (and thank the moles for the free fertilizer they leave behind) or check for excessive grubs. If there are 10 or more grubs per square foot of sod, then you've got a problem. Get rid of the grubs and the moles will move on. See Chapter 9 for ideas on organic grub control.

Chipmunks

These little guys are very adept at making tunnels through the garden. While they're burrowing, they uproot plants and create air pockets that can fill with water and freeze during the winter months. Though they will occasionally eat a few bulbs, their main damage is caused by the tunneling, and even that is minor. You can trap them with live traps if need be or simply fill in the burrows and re-settle any plants they have been disturbed. Try to think of them as part of the ecosystem of the garden and enjoy their antics.

ADVANCED QUICK TIPS

❧ pH AND MORE ❧

Testing

Home pH testers are available at most nurseries for very reasonable prices. To get an accurate measurement from these gizmos you must test several areas of the garden and then average all the readings together.

Changing pH

Time for a pH change in the garden? Choosing the appropriate organic matter can help. If you need to make your soil more acidic, use peat moss; more alkaline, use mushroom soil. Retest your pH the following season to see if the amendments made an effective change.

What is your soil's CEC?

The CEC (cation exchange capacity) of soil refers to its ability to attract and hold certain nutrients. Soils with a high CEC are usually also high in organic matter; soils with a low CEC allow most of the nutrients to leach out. Most laboratory soil tests will inform you of the CEC and some now even tell you the organic matter content.

❧ MICROBES, FUNGI AND RED WRIGGLERS ❧

More essential nutrients

To encourage healthy soil, recruit those microbes! Most chemical fertilizers contain only nitrogen, phosphorus, and potassium (often referred to as N, P, and K); but microbes and plants need more than that to survive. Trace elements (like boron, magnesium and others) are present in quality organic matter and these are just as important as the big N, P, and K. You can also purchase extra soil life in the form of mycorrhiza fungi. These naturally occurring fungi help plants acquire nutrients and fight off bad bacteria.

Worm castings

Raising worms can be very rewarding. It's a great way to get kids involved in the garden. Poke holes in both the lid and base of a large plastic storage bin. Layer the bin with shredded newspaper and kitchen scraps. Introduce red wrigglers (usually purchased by mail order) and watch them work their magic. In a few weeks you'll have a bin full of nutrient-dense worm castings to use in your garden and containers. When you empty the bin for use, simply save a large coffee can of the "soil" and add it to a newly started batch. There are usually enough worms and eggs in it to establish a new population.

✄ COMPOSTING ✄

Trenching

If you don't have the space for an official compost bin, try the burial method. Dig trenches in the garden and bury your kitchen scraps and grass clippings in them. By next season, this material will have decomposed and you can plant your tomatoes right on top of it. You'll notice a definite increase in the earthworm population too!

Jump-starting your next batch

Each time you spread finished compost from your own bin, save a wheelbarrow of the completed product. When you begin your next batch, sandwich this between layers of fresh yard waste for quicker cooking. Just a few shovels can mean millions of non-union microbes working just for you!

Warning on bulk topsoil

Never use bagged or bulk topsoil as an amendment. Often stripped from farm fields, it not only has a low nutrient content, but may contain herbicides or pesticides. Topsoil can also contain noxious weed seeds or root pieces of perennial weeds. If you do need to add topsoil to create a raised bed or level off a particular area in the garden, allow it to sit unplanted for a few months. This will give the soil time to settle and will also permit any weed seedlings to be easily removed. For new bed preparation, we recommend mixing the topsoil with compost and mushroom soil in equal parts.

Manure and weeds

All manure is not created equal. Chicken and sheep manure are very concentrated and should be used only in small amounts to prevent foliage burn. Cow and horse manure are widely available, but full of weed seeds. Remember that all animal waste should be allowed to rest for at least 90 days before using it on the garden. Better yet, add it to the compost pile first.

Save the needles

Fallen pine needles make wonderful mulch for acid loving plants like blueberries, Rhododendrons and Azaleas. As they decompose they will slightly acidify the soil and help build its structure. Jess loves to rake the needles from under her white pines each fall and spread them around her blueberries.

✄ TURNING OLD SOD AREAS INTO HEALTHY SOIL ✄

The layering method

Creating a new garden bed where sod once existed can be a challenging project. Patient gardeners might find success using this layering method. Lay newspaper, about 20 to 25 sheets thick, on top of the sod; then pile on several inches of grass clippings, shredded leaves, compost and other organic matter. Allow the whole heap to sit and decompose for a few months. The sod will eventually die and the organic matter will rot, making tilling for new plantings a piece of cake.

4

THE BENEFITS OF BENEFICIALS
THE BATTLE OF THE BUGS

In gardens, beauty is a by-product.
The main business is sex and death.
— SAM LLEWELYN

We all know the benefits of having bees, butterflies and moths in the garden; most of us learned about pollination in the second grade. But you might not know about all the other insects in the garden whose presence is invaluable. In this chapter we'll discuss how to get these "good bugs" to help you maintain a pest-free garden.

Fight the Good Fight – the nature of the garden

Our gardens are under attack every day. While it's true that your battle with that hungry groundhog or gopher may seem to be the most pressing issue, there's a miniature war being waged in the garden. You might not see them, but aphids are hatching, sawfly larvae are chewing and flea beetles are making perfect, round holes in eggplant leaves; sounds frightening doesn't it? But take heart; your plants are not fighting the battle alone. They've got some allies in this war, and they're called "beneficial" insects. These critters do an amazing job in the organic garden, eating or laying their eggs on the bad guys. Beneficial insects dispatch the nasties quickly, neatly and naturally.

Your organic garden is filled with living things in hiding that can help combat the troublesome bugs.

Before going organic, the standard response to insect damage may have been to blanket the garden with a poisonous white dust. Not only did this kill the offending insect, but it also wiped out every other bug in sight, thereby interrupting the natural cycle of predator and prey. Understanding this cycle is an integral part of organic growing. As with animals, a particular insect is either predator or prey; it either eats other insects or gets eaten itself. Here's where the cycle part comes in. When prey populations are low, there are very few predators (why produce more progeny when there's very little food around?). Because of the lack of natural predators, the prey insects begin to rapidly reproduce. Suddenly there is abundant food available and so the population of predators increases as well. This increase in predators always follows an increase in prey; unless of course we disrupt the cycle by breaking out the pesticides.

When we kill the prey before the beneficial predators have a chance to move in, our good-guy predators are never allowed their natural population increase and will never have a chance to control the bad guys. To a gardener who understands this cycle, waiting a few days will likely eliminate the need to take any action at all.

In essence, before the introduction of synthetic chemicals, nature took care of business; and in an organic garden we are just giving nature a little extra time to work her magic. A bug will hatch, or pupate, and eat enough of the plant to sustain itself and reproduce; right about the time that bad bug is hitting the plant buffet, the predatory insect is getting ready to pounce.

Bring on the Bugs!

When the garden is free of synthetic insecticides the balance of nature returns and the cycle continues. Most gardeners are already familiar with one of the most common beneficial insects, the ladybug. But there's a long list of other insects that can help in the garden as well. Our job as organic gardeners is to ensure that these beneficial insects find a home in our yard. We can do this by providing them with everything they need to thrive and reproduce.

Companion Planting

Though not true in every case, it's the larval stage of many beneficials that does most of the insect eating, while the adults feed on nectar and pollen. So it's important for us to have nectar sources in the garden along with plenty of prey. If we can keep the beneficial adults in and around the garden, when pest populations explode they will be ready to lay their eggs. The majority of beneficial insects are attracted to plants with clusters of small flowers – plants like dill, fennel, Queen Anne's lace and many common herbs. If you already grow these varieties, head out to the garden on a sunny day and watch all the parasitic wasps hovering around the flowers. These tiny, non-stinging wasps parasitize insects like caterpillars, aphids and tomato hornworms by laying eggs on them; when the eggs hatch, the host insect serves as food for the growing larvae. But just like humans, every insect has different tastes. Below, you'll find a chart listing the most common beneficial insects, along with their main prey species and plants that you should have in the garden to attract them.

List of "Good Bugs"	What they battle	What to plant
Tachinid flies	they parasitize caterpillars, beetle and fly larvae	lemon balm, parsley, chamomile
Lacewings	scale, aphids, mites, soft-bodied insects	angelica, tansy, dill, yarrow, Cosmos
Parasitic wasps	whiteflies; moth, beetle and fly larvae, aphids, tomato hornworms	lemon balm, parsley, oregano, dill, sweet alyssum, statice, Cosmos
Ground beetles	slugs, small caterpillars and grubs	amaranth
Ichneumon wasp	various caterpillars	dill
Ladybugs	aphids, mites	dill, morning glory, Queen Anne's lace, yarrow
Damsel bugs (Nabidae)	insect eggs	fennel
Aphidius wasp	aphids	lupine, yarrow, sunflowers
Beneficial mites	thrips, spider mites, fungus gnats	sunflowers, daisies, chamomile
Hoverflies	aphids, mealybugs	alyssum, statice, Cosmos, mint, wild mustard
Pirate bugs	thrips, aphids, mites, scales, whiteflies	daisies, sunflowers
Praying mantis	many crawling insects	tall grasses left over winter
Spiders	many insects	many plants, which serve as shelter
Robber flies	grasshoppers, wasps and other flies	many plants, especially mint

Along with nectar sources, you'll need to provide these bugs with some habitat. One example would be planting ornamental grasses or other plants that will stand all winter near or in the veggie garden. These types of plants tend to be where praying mantises lay their egg cases – spongy, light brown masses.

Hummingbirds are one of the most lovely summer garden sights. This bird is visiting a Tithonia blossom. Other attractor plants include red Salvia, trumpet vine, petunia, Cosmos, Penstemon and cardinal flower. ***Note:*** *Throughout our book you'll see that we have capitalized some plant names and not others. This is because the first word of a plant's proper botanical name – its genus – is always capitalized. Common names are not. Sometimes a plant's genus and common name are the same (like Zinnia and Hosta), so for the sake of consistency we've chosen to capitalize these as well.*

Many varieties of cherry tomatoes (like 'Snow White') are more resistant to blights. Plus, they are prolific producers; sometimes we can barely keep up. Plant a few with your beefsteak and paste tomatoes for plenty of fresh eating.

Don't kill a tomato hornworm if you see white sacks on its back. These parasitic wasp eggs will hatch, feed on the hornworm and then morph into another generation of pest-eating predators. Check out Chapter 4 for more information on these non-stinging wasps and other beneficial insects.

The larval stage of many common butterflies can be found feeding on garden plants and trees. If you find a caterpillar, be sure to identify it before taking any action – you don't want to harm any of these beautiful pollinators.

Design your vegetable garden with accessibility and practicality in mind. Grass paths are easy to mow while 4-foot-wide beds allow the gardener to easily reach the center. Don't forget those cups of beer for luring pepper-eating slugs to certain demise!

Raised beds do not need to be fancy. Simple concrete block does the job; cheap and sturdy. Kids can find all kinds of fun activities in the garden – from beetle collecting to potato digging.

Deer can be a challenge for all gardeners. To deter them, grow plants with highly fragranced or fuzzy foliage. Contact your local cooperative extension agency for a list of deer-resistant plants for your area.

Try different varieties in the veggie patch. 'Easter Egg' radishes look beautiful and taste divine.

Make sure your children spend plenty of time in the garden. Doug's boys grew up on fresh green beans and ripe tomatoes – you should see how tall those boys are now!

For the best garden path, lay down 10 sheets of wet newspaper then cover it with straw. It makes for easy walking, and keeps the boots clean.

Don't forget to maximize the vertical space in your garden. It's easy to grow pole beans, snap peas or cucumbers up your protective fencing. Just train them as they grow.

You should also allow a patch of grass near the veggie garden to go wild, as lacewings like to lay their eggs along grass blades. Lacewing eggs appear in rows along the blade's edge; they are small, oval-shaped eggs that are placed on the end of 1/4-inch filaments, like little lollipops in a row.

Gardeners can even match a host plant to a pest. Plants like sweet alyssum attract Aphidius wasps that attack aphids. So if you've got regular aphid troubles on your roses or tomatoes, under-plant them with sweet alyssum. Or, if every season you have Magnolia scale, plant yarrow next to the tree to attract lacewings. You are essentially bringing in the police before the looters arrive.

Using companion plants as living mulch is another way to get those beneficials to stick around. Thyme, chamomile, small leafed oregano or white Dutch clover planted in your garden's paths attract beneficials (and pollinators) and reduce weeds, instead of using bark, grass or gravel. Plant alfalfa, red clover or another crop under your taller veggies; it will serve as a cover crop over the winter, and as a living mulch and beneficial attractor during the growing season.

Besides luring the good bugs to the garden by providing a proper habitat, these insects can also be bought commercially and then released into the garden. Though we've only had moderate success with this method, others swear by it and it certainly can't hurt. The most popular bug on the market is the ladybug; lacewings and mantis are close seconds. Releasing these insects into the garden does not ensure that they will actually stay there, but if there's plenty of food available they will be more likely to hang around.

Free them at dusk in a well-watered area of the garden. Another trick is to cover the pest-ridden plants with a floating row cover (a lightweight spun fabric that rests on top of the plants) and release the beneficials underneath it; this keeps them captive until the pests are reduced.

You can also now purchase microscopic beneficial nematodes by the millions (these guys really work!). They are added to water and then sprinkled at the base of affected plants or watered into the lawn. These good nematodes prey upon various insects like borers, grubs, cutworms and flea beetles, among others. For a list of sources for purchasing beneficial insects, see the Friends of the Organic Gardener appendix.

Recent Beneficial Research

For us, the most exciting news about beneficial insects comes from ongoing studies at Pennsylvania State University. Scientists there have discovered some amazing stuff about the connections plants have with these good bugs. Plants release many different volatile compounds (odors) into the air; it's their way of communicating with their surroundings. These compounds serve as chemical signals to other plants and to insects. When a plant is being attacked by an insect, say a caterpillar, it releases a specific compound that lures the species of beneficial insect most likely to prey upon the caterpillar. What's even more amazing is that a slightly different compound is released depending on the exact species of caterpillar attacking the plant. The plant is sending an SOS to the beneficials. They've also discovered that plants will release certain compounds when under attack, essentially letting neighboring plants know that it's time to raise their defenses.

What these studies are telling us is that the connection between plants and beneficial insects is quite intricate. They are linked in a symbiotic relationship that has developed over millions of years. It's time for gardeners to recognize the importance of this association and allow it a place in the garden.

A Bit of Useful Advice

When left to their own devices, beneficial predatory insects will do a great job keeping the bad guys in check. Remember, *not every insect needs to be dispatched*. If a plant has only a few aphids on it there is no need to worry, the beneficials aren't far behind; but there may be times when our insect helpers can't keep up and we are forced to step in. If a plant is infested to the point that predators aren't able keep up, it is essential that we find a solution that will eliminate the bad guys without harming our helpers. Many of the organic solutions we offer in Chapter 9 are formulated to allow the beneficials to remain unscathed. Note: Pay close attention to any label instructions warning of potential harm to beneficials. Products with such warnings should be used only as a last resort and only if no other solution can be found.

By allowing nature to run its course, encouraging the predator-prey cycle and understanding natural connections, we enable the garden to stand up for itself – giving us more time to pick tomatoes, plant a late crop of lettuce or just admire our handiwork.

Doug Tells All   *about one heck of a bug*

It was an amazing sight: a big scary-looking wasp, with what appeared to be a 4-inch-long stinger, sitting on a tree trunk. My kids and I had come across one here and there over the years, and that stinger had always sent shivers down our spines. This time, as we sat and watched it, we realized that the long stinger wasn't a stinger at all: that bug was laying eggs with it. Then one day while reading Organic Gardening magazine, I saw a picture of the insect. It was an adult parasitic wasp. Even though it looked menacing, this was actually a friendly bug that would never hurt me and would certainly help the garden.

It was another epiphany for me, and it reinforced my new-found "organic" thinking. Instead of assuming that every insect was bad, I needed to learn the difference between what was helping my garden and what was hurting it.

During those pre-Internet days, gardening information came from books and magazines. I pored over many glossy color photos, recognizing some of the insects from my own garden. I read about ants farming aphids for their sweet honeydew and learned the difference between striped and spotted cucumber beetles. But more importantly, I was drawn into the garden on hands and knees to witness nature's wonderful balancing act. And ironically, what I learned there was something I should have known all along: a garden can not only survive without chemicals, it can thrive.

Jess Tells All | *about herbal harmony*

When I designed my vegetable garden a few years ago I knew it had to include lots of herbs. I use them to cook, to garnish, to dry and to accent my homemade bars of soap. What I came to realize was that by situating my herb patch smack in the center of my garden, I created a wonderful little oasis.

My herb plants are constantly buzzing with tiny wasps, bees, butterflies and hover-flies. I have the central garden bed planted with thyme, oregano (both Greek and Italian), sage, chives, dill, cilantro, chervil, rosemary, parsley (flat and curly) and basil.

I know that by allowing the herbs to bloom I risk altering the taste of the foliage, so I've developed a nice little system that allows me to both harvest the plant stems and reap the benefits of the blooms: from early May through the end of June, I regularly cut bunches of the perennial herbs (oregano, thyme, sage, chives, rosemary). I use them fresh or hang them to dry. After June, I stop harvesting and allow the perennial varieties to bloom. By this time my annual herbs (basil, parsley, cilantro, dill) are just beginning to be large enough to use.

Because the seed of these annual herbs is so inexpensive, I always grow extra. By doing this, I can be assured I'll have plenty to use and plenty to attract those beneficials.

I also interplant many of my garden beds with cutting flowers (sunflowers, amaranth, Cosmos, and Zinnias) and have found that the good bugs enjoy the nectar and pollen of these beauties as well.

QUICK TIPS

❧ BUG INFO ❧

Aphid mummies

Next time you find a colony of aphids on a plant, get out a hand lens and carefully examine them. If you see empty aphid casings (exoskeletons) that have little round holes with an open lid on their backs, you know you have a healthy population of Aphidius wasps in the garden. The wasp larvae eat the inner fleshy part of their aphid host then chew open a lid and emerge as an adult.

Hornworm "eggs"

When you find a hornworm on your 'maters, carefully examine it before removing it from the plant. If you find white, oval eggs hanging off its back, the worm has been parasitized by wasps. It stops feeding shortly after the eggs are laid, so it's no longer a threat to your tomatoes. If you kill it, the eggs will not hatch and your garden will be robbed of another generation of these beneficial wasps. Just leave the hornworm alone.

Spiders

Though they may seem a bit intimidating, spiders are right at home in an organic garden. They are very good at catching grasshoppers, leafhoppers and many other insects. When you find a web or tunnel in the garden be sure to mark it with a survey flag to avoid damaging it.

Mantis alert

While praying mantises are considered beneficial insects, be warned that they don't discriminate. They will eat ladybugs and bees just as quickly as grasshoppers and squash bugs.

✂ REMOVAL TECHNIQUES ✂

Handpicking
Hand removal of pests ensures that no harm will come to any beneficials. If pest numbers reach dangerous levels before the predatory beneficial insects arrive, simply handpick part of the population. This will reduce their numbers to tolerable levels, but still allow some prey to remain for the arriving army.

Blown away
A sharp blast from the garden hose will send aphids and spider mites to the ground, making it hard for them to try and climb back up onto the plant.

That sucks
A battery powered hand vacuum works great at sucking up insects and will put quite a dent in their population.

Ladybug intruders
When ladybugs find their way into your house each fall, use them to your advantage. Gather them in a bowl and take them back out to the garden. They will likely find a new place to hibernate under debris or in the garden shed. You can also place a few on houseplants or the over-wintering tropicals now on your windowsills. Doug takes them out to his greenhouse.

Slugfest
Most kids love any excuse to be up past bedtime — and to play with a flashlight. If slugs are your nemesis, arm the kids with latex gloves, a paper cup and a few extra batteries; show them what slugs look like and where they are likely to find them. Slug hunts used to draw all the neighbor kids to Jess' mom's garden every summer. 'Course the popsicles didn't hurt either.

✠ A POSITIVE ID ✠

Identity issues
Go to the library and find a book that can help you identify beneficial insects. Yes, some of these insects may look a bit scary (think praying mantis), but know your allies. This may help lessen some of the worry that comes when you find a creepy-crawly you aren't familiar with.

Lady larvae
Since ladybug larvae are heavy-duty aphid consumers, it's important to be able to identify them. They look like miniature alligators and are dark grey with red markings. Get to know them; they are about as beneficial as you can get!

Lacewing larvae
These immature insects look a lot like ladybug larvae, except they are light brown with pale markings around their margins. They also have large, curved mandibles. Their favorite foods include aphids, mealybugs, mites and scale.

✠ WHAT TO PLANT ✠

Seed blends
A few organic product catalogs offer seed blends that consist of plants known to attract beneficials. If you have an extra area in the garden that can be a little wild, why not give them a try? We think a basic wildflower blend would help too.

Plant this
Other favorite plants for attracting beneficials include: Calamintha, purple coneflowers, Angelica, asters, yarrow, bee balm, chervil, Joe Pye weed and wild mustard.

Bloomin' bushes

Flowering shrubs can be both a food and shelter source for beneficials. Try elderberry, sweetspire, Clethra, Vitex and Viburnum.

Interplanting

We really feel that planting nectar sources throughout the veggie garden is one of the easiest ways to naturally reduce pests. Mix flowers between your broccoli and put an herbal edging around your beds. Our favorites include daisies, common thyme, feverfew, sage, chives and cilantro. Harvest the herbs, of course, but also allow them to bloom.

Underplants

Don't be afraid to use blooming annual ground covers as a carpet under any susceptible plants. Sweet alyssum, chamomile, nasturtiums, and globe amaranth will not only help draw in the good guys, but will shade the soil and choke out weeds.

Dill

For us, there is one plant that stands above all others for attracting beneficials: dill. It's one of the easiest plants to grow and once it's gone to seed your garden will always have the plants popping up each summer. Dill attracts a plethora of beneficial insects including parasitic wasps, hoverflies and lacewings; and it tastes pretty good with pickles too! The herb is also reported to repel aphids and spider mites. Some gardeners sprinkle it on the ground near squash plants to foil the squash bugs.

✂ WEEDS GONE WILD ✂

Capable clover

Allow white clover to grow in your lawn. Not only will it provide nitrogen to help keep your grass green, but it will draw tons of beneficials to the yard.

Bloomin' weeds

Yes, we're going to go out on a limb here and tell you to let some of your weeds bloom: bloom, mind you, not go to seed. Thistle, goldenrod, clover, lady's thumb and veronica are just a few of the weeds whose flowers attract beneficials. Let them flower, then pull or mow them before the seeds are formed.

ADVANCED QUICK TIPS

✂ LOVE TO LEARN ✂

Beneficials go to school

We have been told that many elementary school science curriculums now include information about using beneficial insects to control pests. Isn't it great that our kids will have an understanding of these natural cycles?

Label law

Many pesticides, most conventional and a few organic, may harm beneficials. Be very careful to read the label in its entirety. If the product is potentially dangerous for beneficial insects it will be clearly stated. If you have to use these products, do so only when there are no beneficials present.

✂ DOWN ON THE FARM ✂

Farming insects

When you encounter a colony of aphids or scale, keep an eye out for ants and yellow jackets. Aphids and scale excrete a sweet, sticky substance called honeydew, and the larger insects actually "farm" them. When you see this farming taking place, know that you may need to take action. Many beneficials will not risk being attacked by the ants or wasps.

Yummy stuff

We recently came across a new product that you can use to help draw in the beneficials. It's a commercially made paste consisting of Brewer's yeast, honey and powdered milk. You apply it to wooden stakes placed throughout the garden and it serves as a food source when nectar levels are low. We haven't tried it, but it sounds interesting.

Backyard barnyard

If you've got the room, chickens and ducks consume copious amounts of garden pests, as well as ticks and mosquitoes. Ducks feast on slugs and it's great fun to watch a good game of chicken football when cabbage loopers are tossed into the chicken run.

✄ OTHER GOOD GUYS ✄

Dragonflies

If you have a pond or wetlands in your garden, you probably already have dragonflies. Create a buffer zone of 3 to 4 feet around your pond by allowing wildflowers and bog plants to grow un-mown. This will provide habitat and marginal areas for dragon and damsel flies to perch and lay their eggs. They eat huge numbers of mosquitoes and other flying garden pests.

Earthworms

Though they aren't officially insects, earthworms are yet another example of beneficial wildlife. They process and aerate the soil, releasing nutrients and leaving behind rich castings. While you can purchase worms for indoor worm-composting bins, we don't recommend adding the worms themselves to the garden. Some of the species for sale aren't native and will not survive the winter. Your best bet is to add plenty of organic matter to your soil – with food that good, your native worms are sure to thrive *and* multiply!

Short on honey

Honeybee populations are finally on the increase after many years of decline. When you come across honeybees in the garden, thank them for their remarkable work. Unless you are allergic, don't be overly afraid of these guys; they will only sting when threatened.

The bees have it

Plant a garden filled with flowers that will attract native bees in addition to European honeybees. Leafcutter, bumble, sweat and digger bees are just a few of our native species. Try growing tickseed, bee balm and goldenrod near crops that you'd like to pollinate. These native bees don't travel far from their nests, so planting nectar sources close to vegetables is a terrific way to lure them in.

Canned bees

You can buy orchard mason bees in a can. The cylinder contains both adult bees and nesting tubes and you simply hang it up in the garden. Docile mason bees are perfect pollinators for the orchard and veggie patch. They will not harm people and are native to most of the U.S.

Nocturnal helpers

Don't forget about bats. They consume an enormous number of flying insects every night and are great for the garden. Put up a wooden bat box on a sheltered wall of the house or shed and, if you have some acreage, allow a few dead trees (snags) to stand. These provide nesting and roosting sites for the flying acrobats.

✖ BAD GUYS ✖

Invasive insects

On the flip side of beneficial insects are invasive ones. Exotic species that were introduced either purposefully or accidentally are finding their way into our fields and forests and often wreaking havoc. Though many introduced species are not a threat, some are posing a major problem to both plants and native insect species. Familiarize yourself with exotics like the Asian long-horn beetle and the emerald ash borer. That way, if you ever come across one, you can report it to the Department of Agriculture and they can act accordingly.

5

Organic Ornamentals

GROWING FLOWERS, SHRUBS AND MORE

In the spring, at the end of the day, you should smell like dirt.
— Margaret Atwood

Ornamentals are the core of most gardens, and they are often where we find the greatest pleasure. The trees and shrubs, annuals and perennials we plant can lift the spirits and provide a respite from our hectic lives. Though we appreciate them mostly for their beauty, ornamentals can raise property values, reduce cooling costs, decorate our lives and offer us endless free therapy. In this chapter we'll explain just how easy it is to grow them organically.

Picking for Perfection – making smart plant choices

We all want our gardens to be lush, thriving *and* low-maintenance. We want to create a beautiful garden that does not become a chore. Choosing appropriate plants is the first step, so prepare to spend some time scouring catalogs, walking through your favorite nursery and asking gardening friends about their favorites. There is an almost infinite variety of plants to choose from, and making smart choices will make all the difference in your maintenance needs down the line.

Plant breeders work tirelessly to create disease-resistant varieties; in fact it's one of their primary goals. Each season a new batch of plants is introduced touting improved disease resistance. It makes great sense from both a gardening and a marketing standpoint: if a certain plant is not prone to disease, we are more likely to buy it. Heck, we'll buy anything that might make our lives easier! An example of recent plant breeding advances can be seen in common garden Phlox. Phlox is known to be susceptible to powdery mildew (a rarely fatal condition, but unattractive nonetheless), and its leaves become gray and mottled. Organic gardeners no longer need to reach for the homemade fungicide to take care of the problem; we now have new varieties that won't get the disease in the first place. It's always good to keep an eye out for "new and improved" choices.

Whether it's fruit trees, flowering shrubs, ground covering perennials or festive annuals – buy plants that will be good at fending for themselves. Instead of choosing ornamentals based on flower color or habit alone, select for ease of maintenance and suitability to your climate.

Native plants have recently become valued landscape specimens, and rightly so. They are tough and adaptable; and since native plants are perfectly suited for the climate and soils of your region, they require very little care. There is a lot of beauty in these plants, and you might be surprised to know that some of your favorite varieties are in fact native. In the eastern U.S. there is beautiful red columbine, wild hydrangea with milky white flowers, and cardinal flower with those luminescent scarlet spires. In the West it's colorful California poppies, frothy grasses and a multitude of brightly colored, drought-resistant desert plants. Your neighborhood nursery will carry some natives for sure, and most cities have a few nurseries that specifically deal in natives. It will be worth your time to seek out these special places and employ their expertise.

Intelligent Design – planning your garden to avoid pest problems

Once you have selected the best and hardiest varieties to fill your garden, your thoughts should turn to design. Create a garden in which every plant is situated in a place where it will shine and thrive. Deciding which plant goes where is as important for the garden as the organic matter you add.

Put the right plant in the right place: this means everything from positioning more tender plants in a sheltered setting to making sure the shrubs aren't planted under the eaves of the house where they wouldn't get the advantage of rainwater.

It's important to learn the cultural needs of the ornamentals you want in your garden. Planting a variety that needs full sun in partial shade isn't going to give you the results you want. By giving plants a proper home, the odds favor your success. It's always easier to match the plant to the area instead of trying to change the garden environment for the plant. That's not to say you shouldn't experiment; it's surprising how adaptable plants can be. Many gardeners enjoy the challenge of discovering which plants will thrive in areas they wouldn't traditionally be planted in. If the experiment doesn't work, simply dig up the plant and try it somewhere else.

Spacing is an important element in your landscape design. When adding a plant to the garden, be sure to place it far enough away from other plants to allow for full growth and to assure proper air circulation. Do some investigating and find out how big it's going to be at maturity, then space accordingly. When plants have room to breathe, their immune systems function better because there is little competition for sunlight, nutrients and water. But space them too closely and those intimate quarters can speed the spread of disease, providing the perfect environment for hosts of insects.

Sometimes, though, no matter how hard you try, a plant just never takes off. When this happens, it's better to cut your losses. We recommend giving plants a few seasons to adjust. If they are still struggling despite several relocations, it's off to the compost pile with them. Don't feel guilty about this – it happens to all of us.

When you're making all these choices about what goes where, give serious thought to accessibility – you've got to get into that garden and maintain those plants. If a shrub is surrounded by a thick bed of tall flowers, it's going to be tough to get in there and prune. Good accessibility will simplify maintenance. Many gardeners will design their plantings with small "worker" paths to allow easy interior access. It's also important to be able to enjoy the garden with friends and family, so when you're planning paths meant to usher guests through the garden, allow enough room for two people to walk side by side, enjoying what you've created.

What YOU Do Matters! – organic cultural practices

Cultural practices are any efforts you make to manipulate a plant or its environment – actions like pruning, staking, garden cleanups, fertilizing and deadheading (more on that in a bit). These are a part of everyday garden maintenance and if not performed correctly, they can greatly affect the strength of your plants. In managing your ornamentals organically, knowing *how* you accomplish these tasks can mean the difference between healthy, flourishing plants and disease-ridden, overgrown monsters.

Pruning – an integral tool for keeping the garden healthy and making plants behave. It's done for several reasons: to remove dead wood, control size, increase fruit production, improve flowering, maintain shape or train growth. Timing is everything: prune a shrub at the wrong time and you might just lose your blooms for the season or be lopping off potential fruit. Shrub pruning is timed according to whether the plant blooms on old wood (last year's growth) or new wood (growth that has occurred during the current season). Old wood bloomers are pruned immediately after flowering, while new wood bloomers are pruned in fall, winter or early spring.

If you aren't sure which kind of wood a particular shrub blooms on, here's a good rule of thumb: if it blooms before June 15th it's likely blooming on old wood; after June 15th, it's new wood.

We've included the pruning chart below to guide you in deciding when it's the right time to prune certain specimens. The exception: any dead wood you find can be pruned out whenever discovered, despite the season.

Plant class	Examples	When to prune
Shrubs, old-wood bloomers	Azalea, Rhododendron, Pieris, laurel, Forsythia, quince, Hydrangea macrophylla, lilac, witch hazel, dogwood, honeysuckle, Viburnum, Wisteria, Weigela	Immediately after bloom
Shrubs, new-wood bloomers	Hydrangea arborescens and paniculata, Spirea, beautyberry, Vitex, smoke bush, Abelia, Aralia, snowberry, coralberry	Fall, winter or early spring
Fruit trees	Apple, pear, peach, apricot, persimmon, plum, cherry, blueberry	Late winter
Herbaceous perennials	Many species	Late fall or early spring
Woody perennials (those not considered shrubs)	Caryopteris, butterfly bush, Russian sage	Late winter or early spring
Ornamental grasses	Many species	Late winter or early spring
Evergreen trees and shrubs	Hollies, pines, spruces, boxwood, Arborvitae, juniper	Late spring or winter
Most deciduous trees	Many species except those listed below	Winter
Deciduous trees known as "bleeders" (because of excess sap loss)	Maple, birch, elm, walnut	Mid-summer or late fall

Before you start, have a plan and a reason to prune, and know what results to expect. If you're hoping to open up and rejuvenate an old lilac, be prepared to remove some of the larger branches to the ground; but if your goal is to keep your boxwood in a tight, compact form, then you'll want to remove only the topmost few inches of each branch. This will encourage every cut stem to grow two new shoots, leading to thicker, denser growth. When pruning shrubs or trees it's important to take your time and look at them from a distance after each cut to ensure you're not overdoing it. Research the growth habit of shrubs, as well as the ideal way to prune them – before you break out the saw.

A word of caution: it's possible that improper pruning can open the plant up to attack by pests and disease, or lead to excessive moisture loss and slow healing. Be sure to keep your pruning equipment clean. Disease can be readily spread by a contaminated pair of pruners. You can disinfect tools with a quick swab of rubbing alcohol or hydrogen peroxide.

Before beginning any major pruning work on your trees, we recommend having a certified arborist take a look. Trees are major investments, and it's worth spending a few extra dollars to ensure your investment is treated with respect. Most local tree companies will have at least one certified arborist on staff, so be sure to ask for credentials. Check out the Quick Tips section for more advice on tree care.

Deadheading – a seasonal (and indispensable) garden task. This is the simple act of removing spent flowers to promote new growth and to stimulate further flower production. Deadheading will keep annual flowers blooming their best and help certain perennials re-bloom. The more you deadhead, the more flowers the plant will produce. In a way, you are fooling nature; a plant devotes a lot of energy into producing progeny and once that flower begins to go to seed, it thinks its job is done and stops producing flowers. But when we remove those potential seeds, the plant keeps churning out flowers in hopes of eventually producing some seed.

Not all plants respond to deadheading; you can remove every spent blossom on a peony, but it will be to no avail. Peonies are just one variety of plant that blooms only once each season. But deadhead that butterfly bush, Salvia, or Phlox and chances are, you'll get another flush of gorgeous blooms. Because deadheading can be a tedious job, plant breeders are beginning to develop some varieties that will re-bloom without any effort on our part. Some newer varieties of petunias carry this trait.

Every flower is deadheaded in a different manner. Marigolds can be pinched off at the flower's base, while dahlias should be cut back all the way to the main stem. Yarrow is cut clear to the foliage tuft at ground level and coneflowers are removed as far back as the next flower bud. If you aren't sure exactly how far back to cut when you deadhead, a safe bet is to follow the flower stem back to the first set of leaves and cut it just above that site. There are specific, detailed deadheading guides available in many basic gardening books and we recommend finding one for your needs.

Mulching – another essential seasonal job in your ornamental garden beds. In Chapter 3 we paid a lot of attention to the subject of mulching. We illustrated the best techniques and materials to use for different garden areas and explained why this chore is so important. We urge you to revisit Chapter 3 each season to re-familiarize yourself with the subject.

Watering – Even those well-mulched beds will occasionally dry out. In this book we talk a lot about watering, and this important cultural practice is the same for ornamentals as it is for most other plants: they do best with about 1 inch of water a week. Keep in mind that this is just a general rule of thumb. There are many times when our gardens will get several weeks of consistent moisture followed by a dry spell. Because the plants are healthy, deep-rooted and well maintained, they need not always be watered during a brief dry period. It's only during prolonged times without rain that we feel the need to lug out the sprinklers. And even then it's only necessary for newly planted trees and shrubs, or shallow-rooted perennials and annuals.

Propagation 101 – Makin' Babies

One of the most rewarding aspects of gardening is the ability to share the fruits of our labor with others. This can mean both the literal fruits, in the form of an extra zucchini, a colander of ripe tomatoes or a bushel of apples, and also "fruits" in the form of new plants.

Basically, there are two ways to ensure that you'll have more than enough plants to share with gardening friends: you can start them from seed or you can vegetatively propagate your existing plants. The "Seeds 101" section in Chapter 6 teaches you the essentials of beginning new plants from seed. As for vegetative propagation, we'll cover that right here – starting with what the heck vegetative propagation actually means.

It's a term horticulturists use to describe the process of taking an existing "mother" plant and creating new plants from some part of it. Unlike humans, a plant's cells have the ability, no matter what part of the plant they come from, to create a whole new plant. It's called "totipotency" and it means every plant cell contains all the genetic information necessary to create a plant that is an exact clone of the mother. For us, if we lose an arm there is no way our body can grow a new one; our cells just can't do it. Plants, on the other hand, can grow new roots or shoots whenever necessary. Some do it more readily than others and some have very unique ways of making their own babies by actually "re-programming" some of their cells.

Plants can be vegetatively propagated several ways. For many perennial plants, the easiest way to do this is through **crown division**. This simply means digging up the clump and chopping it into pieces. As long as each segment has both a root system and a shoot system, the division will go on to become a healthy new plant. It will be genetically identical to the mother plant, and as long as the division is done properly and the new plant is cared for, the chances of success are great. Crown division works well for daylilies, Hosta, ornamental grasses, Veronicas, Phlox, shasta daisies and many other common clump-forming perennials.

Another way to easily propagate many perennial plants is by taking advantage of the natural propagation they already perform. A lot of plants spread themselves by creating horizontal stems called *rhizomes* and *stolons* (think bearded iris, bee balm, Solomon's seal, lily-of-the-valley and goldenrod); or by runners (as in spider plants or strawberries). The plant does this on its own and all we need to do is lop off a section of the plant with a good, sharp shovel and we have a whole new plant.

Then there is the process of taking **cuttings** – either stem, leaf or root. Cuttings can be used to propagate shrubs, perennials and even some annuals. What we are doing in this case is creating a new plant by removing a portion of the mother and encouraging it to grow either a new root system, a new shoot system or, in the case of a leaf cutting, both.

For *stem cuttings*, cut off a portion of a stem about 3 to 4 inches in length. Remove all but the top two leaves, insert the bottom inch of the piece into a rooting hormone (see the Glossary for a quick definition) and then "plant" it into potting soil or vermiculite. Maintain high humidity by placing it, pot and all, in a sealed plastic baggie for a few weeks; then place it in bright, but not direct, sunlight. Keep it well watered and within a month or so most plants will form roots. Some species, especially woody shrubs, require special treatment and timing, so you may find it necessary to investigate the best technique before you begin.

Though *leaf cuttings* can't be preformed with many species, it is fun to try with more succulent varieties – like sedums, African violets or jade plants.

A single leaf is removed from the mother plant, nicked at various spots around the margin and then the edge is rolled in rooting hormone. After doing this, the leaf is pinned flat to the soil's surface (using a piece of bent wire or a few metal hairpins), so all of the cuts are in contact with it, and the humidity is kept high as described above. Whole new baby plants will form where each nick was made and the original leaf eventually rots away. The newly formed plantlets are really cute, but may take quite a long time to reach a substantial size.

Root cuttings – best done with shrubs and thicker rooted perennials like bleeding hearts or Oriental poppies – are created by cutting off a pencil-thick portion of root 2 to 3 inches long and burying it in a tray of sand or vermiculite. Either lay the root pieces flat or be sure to keep track of which end is up – they won't grow if planted upside down. No rooting hormone is necessary for this type of cutting as no new root system needs to develop; the existing system only needs to grow. On average, it will take about four to five weeks for the new shoot system to emerge, though it depends on the time of year and the species you are trying to propagate.

You can propagate woody shrubs through a process known as **layering**. This method allows a new plant to grow while the piece being rooted is still connected to the mother plant. It is performed by bending a low branch of an existing shrub toward the ground, making a shallow 1 inch slice in the bark, dusting the cut with rooting hormone, then pinning or burying the cut portion of the branch in the soil. The injured area will form roots within a few months and then the rooted portion can be cut from the mother plant. Flexible plants like Forsythia or raspberries naturally layer themselves, but the process can be an excellent way to create more shrubs without needing a greenhouse or any special equipment.

For beginners, vegetatively propagating your own garden plants can be an easy way to gain a bit of gardening confidence – each success means the creation of new life. For gardening pros, it means the ability to help those newbie gardeners get their sea legs by sharing the wealth of your own garden, passing along favorites and enjoying the opportunity to try something new.

Jess

Feeding the Masses – fertilizing your ornamentals

Every organic gardener knows the power of compost; we preach to anyone who will listen about all the incredible things compost provides for plants. It is by far the greatest soil additive available. Only 1 inch of compost per year – either applied as a top-dressing or worked into the soil – will provide *all* the nutrients your ornamentals need for a full season's growth. It's pretty amazing stuff.

If you are unable to spread that layer of compost, there are also some organic commercial granular fertilizers available. In Chapter 6 we have a chart listing some of these fertilizers and what they provide. However, you'll note that many of them are not balanced. In other words, their ratio of nitrogen, phosphorus and potassium (N, P and K) isn't proportional. For most ornamentals you'll want to choose a granular fertilizer that has relatively equal amounts of those three nutrients. In our Friends of the Organic Gardener appendix we list many companies that sell quality, balanced organic fertilizers perfectly suited for use on ornamental flowers and shrubs.

It's best to apply granular fertilizers in early spring and then perhaps a light application at the end of summer; but no later than August 15th (fertilizing beyond this date will promote too much tender, frost-sensitive growth). If you do apply a late summer fertilizer, choose one that is low in nitrogen and a bit higher in phosphorus and potassium. This will encourage root growth and enhance the plant's winter hardiness.

Organic granular fertilizers can offer plants a little boost during the growing season, but they are not always necessary. Since we (and now hopefully you) are planting in soil that is rich with organic matter, any excess nutrients we apply will just go to waste (and seep into the ground water). The problem with so many non-organic gardens is that plants have to survive solely on chemical fertilizers, and that's never going to produce the all-round healthy plants that grow in rich, organic soil.

Tucking in the Garden – winterizing for an easier spring

As the season comes to an end it might be tempting to lie back in the recliner, but there's one more important job to do that helps keep the garden free of pests and diseases: a good fall cleanup. When frost brings an end to the gardening year, strip the garden of annual plants and tidy up the perennial border. Compost all healthy refuse from the garden – items like tomato vines and annual plants, overripe veggies and fallen leaves. Don't put this job off because diseases and pests over-winter in debris; and it never hurts to get a jumpstart on spring.

In the vegetable garden you can choose to till the garden in fall, making it easier for planting next season – or you can lay down a blanket of mulch or plant a cover crop (see Chapter 3) to prepare for next year.

In the perennial garden there are two schools of thought on what to do with frosted foliage: one camp cuts the dead stems down and the other allows them to stand for wildlife to eat and take shelter under. Either way is fine; if you can't stand the sight of those brown sticks and wild seedpods, hack them to the ground. If you see winter interest in the contrast of the dark stems against the snow, let them stay. The birds will love you for it. Who knows, they might stick around in the spring to eat their fill of cabbage loopers.

Those annual flowers, though, will need to come out after the first frost of the season. It's easier to get the plants pulled before the frost turns them to mush, but we love to see them bloom as long as possible. Sometimes you'll pull the plants in fear of frost, only to be spared the cold weather; then you've sacrificed an extra week or two of color.

A good leaf cleanup is the last, and maybe most dreaded, job of the season. Collecting them is the hard part, but they can be a very valuable resource for the garden. When leaves break down they create a type of compost called *leaf mold*. This black organic matter is a gardener's dream. And even though some leaves are acidic in nature, when fully rotted they will attain a fairly neutral pH. Even if you just build a huge pile of leaves somewhere on the property, they will eventually break down, providing you with another source of quality homemade organic matter.

If the leaves aren't too thick they can be shredded with the lawn mower and left to break down over the winter. But don't pile whole leaves into the perennial bed; they will form a mat over the plant crowns and cause them to rot. If you're going to mulch with leaves, shred them first and only use them in between plants, never piled on top. Leaves can also be raked, bagged and stored near the compost pile for use in building a new pile next season. There is never a need to send them to a landfill.

If you follow the advice in this chapter, your ornamentals will be in good hands. The secret is to select the best plants, follow proper cultural techniques and keep a close eye on pests and diseases (see Chapter 9). You will be able to create a beautiful, low-maintenance garden filled with dazzling blooms and luscious foliage – easily.

Doug Tells All | *about the dahlia*

The road to the perfect garden is full of many twists and turns. New plants infatuate us; we embrace them, and care for them by learning each of their special needs. But infatuation can only last so long and soon some other amazing bloom or fantastic foliage catches our fancy.

For me, right now, it's dahlias that have captured my heart. It's hard to tell if it's a "till death do us part" relationship, but I can't think of any flower that can compete with those soulful blooms. With some plants reaching 6 feet high, huge flowers in shades of red, white, purple and more; the diversity of dahlias is amazing. Other varieties hug the ground, only reaching 12 inches high, yet prolifically covering their foliage with flowers. And when I take a bunch into work, people walk by asking what all the different flowers are. "They're all dahlias," I say to the awestruck visitor.

Each spring I attend the Greater Pittsburgh Dahlia Society's annual auction. It's one of my favorite days of the season. The auction is held in a small town hall where members bring food for all the participants. We sit on folding metal chairs, our little auction form in hand, dreaming of what those dried brown tubers will reveal by mid-season. The president of the society holds the tubers up, explaining what color they will be and how big they will grow.

But it's when he makes special mention of plants created by one of the society's own members that my interest is really piqued. There's just something about the local connection of these flowers that attracts me: some are named after local towns or streets, but more importantly, they are grown by my neighbors. And even though they might live 50 miles from me and not just across the street, we're bonded by our affection for gardening and dahlias.

Dahlias start to bloom late in the season when most perennials have finished their show and annuals are beginning to tire. It signals a time when most gardeners will be able to rest and recharge. But as frost blackens the foliage, bringing an end to the summer, the dahlias live on in the form of their tubers, nestled into boxes until next spring, when the love affair is ignited once again.

Jess Tells All — *about the rain barrel*

One of the smartest investments I made when installing my front garden was a rain barrel. It is a beautiful, old oak wine barrel that sits at the bottom of our porch's downspout. Because it is in such a prominent place, my husband and I chose an attractive barrel (we paid about $120), but there are certainly less expensive ones on the market. Green or black plastic models are common and many of them have connector options that allow you to attach several barrels together to catch the overflow. Our wine barrel has a hose connector about 6 inches from the ground which makes filling watering cans a breeze (though depending on how full the barrel is, I may have to pull the hose downhill before filling).

An industrious friend went to a local pierogie maker and was given a few 50-gallon plastic barrels once used for cooking oil. She attached her own hose connector and covered the top with hardware cloth to keep out debris. The pierogie maker wanted to send her home with every barrel he had, but she only had so much room in the truck (and so many downspouts!). If you are going to recycle a used plastic barrel like this, make sure it was used for food and not chemicals.

Rain barrels prevent useful water from heading into storm sewers. In my opinion it is a wonderful way to help relieve some of the pressure on our overtaxed storm water management systems. I think every house should have a rain barrel or two.

If you want your own barrel, but the potential for mosquitoes is holding you back, don't let it. There are mosquito dunks made from the natural biological insecticide Bt (you can find more info about Bt in Chapter 9) and I just toss one into the barrel every month or so. You can also use fine screens over the barrel's opening to keep the adult mosquitoes from accessing the water to lay their eggs.

QUICK TIPS

✄ PERENNIALS ✄

Save the love

To save caladium, dahlia and canna tubers, dig them out after frost has blackened the foliage. Knock off the dirt, dry them for a day on newspaper then store them in a box of vermiculite or peat moss at around 50 degrees. Don't store them where temperatures will dip below freezing. Next spring, pot them up; or plant them directly in the garden after the last frost.

Roses are red...

Actually they come in all sorts of colors and varieties. Roses have an unfounded reputation for being fussy (it's really only hybrid teas that fit that bill). Shrub roses grow like weeds and bloom for long periods of time. They are disease-resistant and often have colorful seed pods called hips that provide winter interest. Old-fashioned climbing roses will cover an arbor with flowers in just a few years. There are also many newer varieties that are disease resistant.

Christmas in the garden

If you are growing tender perennials that aren't fully hardy in your zone, you'll need to add a light layer of mulch to protect them through the winter. When you are ready to haul the Christmas tree out of the living room, saw off the boughs and lay them over top of the plants. They are perfect – light enough to allow air to circulate and not crush the plant, but heavy enough to provide ample protection.

✖ SHRUBS ✖

Blooming hydrangeas

In certain parts of the country, it can be tough to get hydrangeas to bloom. To help encourage good flowering, don't cut them back until new buds have formed; and only cut them back to this new growth. Some new varieties, like 'Endless Summer,' bloom on old *and* new growth, giving you more reliable blooms.

Meatball madness

Do not shear shrubs into meatball shapes; it is not their natural growth habit, and it just looks silly.

Four-season shrubs

When shopping for shrubs, look for selections that have more than one season of interest in the landscape. Choose varieties that not only have beautiful flowers, but interesting bark or fall foliage. Shrubs with small fruits, like many Viburnums or beautyberries, can add a lot of color to the winter garden.

✖ COMPOST ✖

Organic pot

Be aware that most commercial potting mixes contain chemical fertilizers. For your lushest, most beautiful container plantings ever, use a fertilizer-free mix; then add a few shovels of compost before planting. These organic mixes can be found at several of the sources listed under Friends of the Organic Gardener.

Air it out

There's a compost aeration tool that helps bring air into the pile. It's a long metal shaft that is stuck into the pile; at the end are two hinged thingamajigs that unfold when you pull it out. It's an easy way to aerate without having to turn the whole pile.

Hot hot hot

A compost thermometer will allow you to monitor the temperature of the pile. The peak of efficiency is at 160 degrees. If your pile isn't getting that hot, don't worry; everything will still rot down, it will just take longer. If you want to raise the temperature, adjust the balance of browns and greens and add a bit of water. Making the pile a bit larger will also help raise the temperature.

Weeds in the compost

When adding materials to the compost pile, avoid weeds that have already gone to seed. Most home compost piles do not get hot enough to kill weed seeds. Have a separate unused dump pile for those.

❧ TREES ❧

Stow the weedwhacker

Be careful when using a power trimmer around trees. The machine can damage bark, encouraging pests and disease and, in some cases, causing death.

Trees need a boost too

Young trees and shallow rooted types like pines and dogwoods will benefit from a layer of compost or an application of organic granular fertilizer each year.

Take me to the top

Never let anyone use a technique called "topping" when pruning your trees. The practice cuts off the top of the tree and is one of the most harmful pruning practices out there. If someone tells you they are going to top the tree, escort them off the property and call a certified arborist.

Dormant volcano

Another technique we see a lot of is the tree volcano. A tree is planted on top of a small manmade hill, then the root ball is covered with mulch. These trees usually don't live long because they dry out quickly and their roots have nowhere to grow. Trees should be planted even with the ground for best results.

Be cool

We all know trees provide shade, but did you know they can save you hundreds of dollars in annual cooling bills? Put a chair under that shade tree and read a book, take a break and enjoy the day.

Natural healing

For years we were told to apply sealing products to tree wounds, but now arborists tell us to let them heal on their own.

Breathe it in

Not only are trees beautiful, but they produce lots of oxygen for us to breathe – which is, of course, a good thing. They may also help protect the garden from early or late frosts by providing a sheltering canopy over smaller plants.

❧ DESIGN TIPS ❧

Designing beds

Use a garden hose as a template to help you visualize the curving edge of a flower bed. Mark the area with stakes, then cut your sod.

One of Doug's favorite garden tools

Nothing makes a bed look better than a freshly cut edge. There's a tool called an edger that looks like a half moon. To use it, push it into the soil like a shovel at a 45-degree angle and remove the dirt.

Shrubs in the border

When designing your perennial bed, plan on incorporating a few shrubs, both blooming and evergreen. They will provide winter interest, summer height and habitat for pest-eating birds.

Bloom time

Since most perennials have a relatively short bloom time, be sure to plant many different varieties: this will ensure you'll have something in flower all season long.

Cover up quick!

Annual vines are great for covering ugly fences or gaining privacy from those nosey neighbors. They are quick growing and many are easy to start from seed. Our favorites include morning glory, moonflower, sweet peas, cypress vine, vining Nasturtium and purple Hyacinth bean.

Summer shrubs

Want more summer flowers from your shrubs? Plant some of these great mid-season bloomers: Clethra, Spirea, Vitex, Potentilla, Caryopteris and Heptacodium.

✂ MAINTENANCE INFO ✂

Folding saw

Buy yourself a small folding pruning saw with a sharp serrated edge. They cut on the pull stroke and glide through the push stroke with ease. Many come with replaceable blades and can cut branches up to 2 inches thick. They are very reasonably priced and fit nicely in your back pocket.

The only time we recommend using electric hedgetrimmers

For gardeners with a lot of ornamental grasses, spring can mean extra work. Taller varieties should be cut to 8 inches each spring before new growth begins. To make quick work of them, shear them with the electric hedgetrimmer, rake the stalks into a pile and run them over repeatedly with the lawn mower. They will be nicely chopped and ready to add to the compost pile.

Shredded tire mulch

Though we're big advocates of recycling, we don't feel that shredded tires make an appropriate garden mulch. They may contain heavy metals and they will never break down to feed the soil. Tire mulch should only be used under playground equipment, if at all.

Wagon wheels

You can purchase expensive metal grow-through staking systems, or you can make your own. If you have perennials that regularly need staking, place four bamboo stakes around the periphery of each clump and one in its center. Wrap jute or hemp twine around and between the stakes creating the image of a wagon wheel. Do this early in the season and allow the flowering stems to grow through it. They will have plenty of support and you can add additional layers of twine as the plants grow.

Here, fishy fishy

For an instant boost, especially for container plantings, try fish emulsion. It's a liquid fertilizer made from fish by-products. A great natural version of those blue chemical liquid fertilizers, fish emulsion will not burn foliage or stain hands.

Over-wintering houseplants

Invest in a few shop lights with fluorescent bulbs to place over your patio plants that you have moved indoors during the colder months. Though the bulbs don't throw the right kind of light to make many blooms, they will help the plants produce new leaves and will keep them green. Watch over-wintering specimens very carefully for aphids, mealybugs and spider mites. These insects often piggyback inside where the warm temperatures can make their populations explode. See Chapter 9 for organic methods to control these pests.

ADVANCED QUICK TIPS

✄ PERENNIAL PLANTS ✄

Long-blooming perennials

We love perennials that have long bloom times, an unusual characteristic in a perennial. Our favorites include: Corydalis lutea, Scabiosa columbaria, Coreopsis grandiflora, Knautia japonica, Salvia x superba, Oreganum vulgare, and Dicentra exima.

Daylilies

After daylilies bloom, cut off the flowering stalks. Cut all the foliage back to the ground when it starts to look ratty; new growth will emerge that is healthy and lush.

Dividing success

Many perennials benefit from being divided every 3 to 4 years; a daunting task for varieties with thicker roots. For difficult divisions, we love a tool called a hori-hori. It's a large, steel-bladed knife with a serrated edge, perfect for hacking those plants in half (or for digging up deep-rooted weeds). Just watch those fingers!

Hormones

Most commercial rooting hormones (used to root plant cuttings) are synthetic. For organic gardeners, that's a no-no. If you want to start your own cuttings, buy a brand that is made from willow bark. Willow has a high concentration of natural auxins – the hormone needed to "force" roots – and this natural choice works just as well as its synthetic counterpart.

Ground covers

With so many interesting ground covers, it's a shame we get stuck in the Pachysandra rut. In warmer climes, we understand it's Gazania that's been overused. For a change, try Epimedium, Tiarella, bearberry, Ajuga, Hypericum or Liriope if you live in colder parts of the country. Where winters are mild and rainfall is sparse, use rosemary or Myoporum to cover barren ground.

✖ TREES ✖

Remembrance trees

Plant a tree for a new addition to the family or to honor someone who's passed. Trees can outlive the gardener who plants them, so it's an investment in the family's future. Choose a tree that means something to you and that you will enjoy looking at for years to come. Great choices to remember someone are redbud, with its heart-shaped leaves and weeping cherry for its name and habit.

Once extinct, now thriving

One of our favorite trees is the dawn redwood. The tree was thought to be extinct, but was discovered in a valley in China in the 1940s. The dawn redwood is a deciduous conifer with beautiful reddish brown bark. It matures at about 100 feet and is a fast grower. Breeders have recently released a variety with chartreuse foliage.

Making the cut

For trimming off large branches, make two cuts. The first cut is made a few inches away from the trunk. If you cut too close to the tree, when the branch separates it could strip off the bark. After the first cut you'll be left with a small nub maybe a few inches long. Make the second cut close to the trunk, leaving about 1/4 inch of the nub. Be sure not to cut too close; that's an invitation for insects and disease.

✄ TOOL TIME ✄

Mail call

Got an area in the garden that's a little distance from the main house? Put an old mail box out there with some hand tools inside. They will stay dry and you'll avoid the hike back to the tool shed if you forget your pruners.

Buying pruners

If there's one piece of equipment not to skimp on, it's a good pair of pruners. Cheap ones will last a season or two, but a quality pair will perform for many, many years. Jess has been using the same pair of Felcos for 15 years. Buy a brand with replaceable parts so when the blade wears out or the spring rusts you can simply replace it instead of buying a whole new pair.

Lost tools

Here are a couple of ideas to keep your tools from getting lost. Paint the handles bright orange (that way when they fall into the compost bin they will be easily found), and buy a tool bag. Available at local nurseries, some bags even incorporate a little folding stool to sit on while weeding the day away.

Pole pruners

If you regularly prune a lot of fruit trees or tall shrubs, invest in a pole pruner. It's a long pole topped with a pulley-powered blade that cuts high branches with ease. Some also have toothed saw blades as well.

THE EVENING GARDEN

Night time is the right time

If you've got a day job and the only time you get to enjoy your garden is at dusk, plant an evening garden. These gardens are filled with plants that exhibit nighttime fragrance and often have white, luminescent blooms. Locate the evening garden very near your outdoor living space so you can spend time enjoying the garden during dinner and a glass of wine. Plants that shine in the evening garden include Datura, moonflower, Nicotiana, Heliotrope, sweet alyssum and Brugmansia.

TROUBLE

Salt

Salt damage from roads, sidewalks and driveways can wreak havoc on both your soil and your plants. For areas that are frequently splashed, build a "fence" of burlap to protect shrubs and trees. Once the salt has entered the soil, you can't take it out. Rainwater and irrigation will eventually dilute it and carry it away, but in the meantime, it can do some major damage. Gardens adjacent to salted areas should be planted with salt tolerant varieties like Clethra, inkberry and Japanese holly, bayberry and beautyberry.

6

THE GARDEN OF EATIN'
VEGGIES AT THEIR BEST!

My garden is an honest place.
— RALPH WALDO EMERSON

Building a vegetable garden can seem intimidating, especially if it's your first. But for centuries gardeners have harvested a bounty of crops by following some basic principles. In this chapter we'll give you lots of ideas on how, where and what to plant in the vegetable garden.

Attractive Asparagus? – designing a vegetable garden with flair

The organic vegetable garden doesn't need to be a utilitarian patch of ground with endless straight rows of beets and corn; it can be a wonderful cornucopia of interesting plants in a variety of designs, limited only by a gardener's imagination. We think a vegetable garden should be a place to discover, relax and reflect (especially while eating warm tomatoes in the summer sun!).

The key to designing any garden is patience. Study the area carefully before beginning to dig. Watch where the sun hits certain spots in the morning and how long it sticks around in the afternoon. Most vegetables need at least 6 hours of full sun, ideally more. Site the garden a substantial distance from any mature trees. This will not only keep the trees from shading your plants but will also prevent those fibrous tree roots from competing with your veggies for both nutrients and moisture. Don't forget that the vegetable garden should also have a place for flowers. They will fill the garden with both beauty and interest, and will attract those ever-important pollinators.

Raised beds – something to consider instead of planting in conventional rows. We have found this method to be easy and handy for all types of gardeners. Raised beds are usually about 4 feet wide, 6 feet long and 16 inches deep, allowing the grower to reach inside without walking on the soil. Of course their ultimate dimensions will depend on the layout of the garden and how the paths are set. You can shape them however you like – we've even seen a garden with a central star-shaped bed. These structures are meant to be permanent, so be sure to take the time to construct them carefully. You can use stone, block, untreated wood (our favorites are cedar, locust and redwood) or fake "lumber."

When you fill the beds with soil, we recommend you mix in plenty of organic matter right from the start; that way you're beginning with the healthiest soil possible.

The perfect ratio is:

    1/3 topsoil
    1/3 compost
    1/3 leaf mold or mushroom soil.

Every spring the soil is turned over, and since it is never compacted by foot or tractor traffic, it will be loose and easy to work. There are many advantages to raised beds, besides increased accessibility. The soil warms earlier in the spring and is often well draining. If you build them a bit higher, you can garden without bending over, and weeding is a breeze.

Make sure your garden's paths are as convenient as the beds themselves. They should be a minimum of 3 feet wide – you'll still need to get that wheelbarrow in there. Simply lay down landscape fabric (available at most garden centers) and cover it with shredded bark or pea gravel. You can also build permanent paths of flagstone or brick. Grass is another option, as are low growing herbs like creeping thyme and chamomile – the fragrance is an added bonus!

Gardening in rows – If you prefer, set the garden up so that the rows run east to west; this will maximize the available light. Space your plants appropriately to ensure they will thrive and to simplify cultivating and harvesting. Rows of lettuce or other small plants would be closer together than rows of tomatoes. If you'd like to add a little interest to a row garden, plant your rows on the bias or mix up the varieties.

Planting in blocks – This works particularly well for veggies that are started from seed, like lettuce, arugula, spinach or Swiss chard. Combining blocks and rows together in the garden can form a patchwork of different textures and colors, while still being convenient for harvesting and maintenance.

Once you've laid out the garden, the next step is making sure you're not feeding the local wildlife. Some vegetable gardens just need chicken wire around the perimeter; others need an 8-foot-tall fortress. If it's just bunnies, the chicken wire will suffice, but if deer are a problem you'll need to build that fortress. Picket or stockade fencing will sometimes discourage deer, as they don't like to jump into enclosed spaces. But if the deer do hop in, we recommend extending the support posts a few feet higher and hanging heavy plastic fencing up to 8 feet high (see the Friends of the Organic Gardener appendix for some fence sources). To discourage burrowing varmints like groundhogs, you'll need to bury your fencing at least 8 inches deep. For this task we suggest renting a ditch-witch from your local equipment dealer and really taking the time to do it right. Those groundhogs can be real buggers!

To Till or Not to Till – preparing the soil

In Chapter 3 we gave you all the information you'll need to prepare your vegetable garden's soil to perform at its best. If you read that chapter (of course you did!) you already know what we're going to tell you to do. Yep, you got it...add that organic matter! For veggies, it's best to use well-aged manure, compost, mushroom soil, leaf mold or any combination of the above. Review the soil amendment chart in Chapter 3 for the digs on each option. The more organic matter you add, the better the soil will become. Remember, ideally you should add a few inches of organic matter each season to replenish the nutrients depleted by your plants.

After you've dumped on the last wheelbarrow of organic matter, you'll need to work it into the soil. There are two schools of thought on how to do this. Your choice depends on how easily the soil can be worked and on your own physical capabilities. Digging by hand is the best method for maintaining good soil structure, but it can be stressful on the back. Rototilling, especially if done when the soil is too wet, can adversely affect soil structure, breaking it down too much. On the upside, rototilling can be quicker and physically easier (especially if you hire the neighbor kid). So, if you've got it in you, dig by hand; if not, break out the tiller.

Top Picks – variety selection

Now that your soil is enriched and prepared, let's get to the fun part – planting! Choosing what to plant can be a dilemma for beginners, but we promise it gets easier and more exciting each year. As your confidence builds, you'll want to try some unusual choices and funky varieties. Ask garden friends about some of their favorite picks, or go to your local nursery and find out what's "in style." The source appendix in the back lists several of our preferred suppliers.

Heirlooms have become popular in the last few years for good reason; they taste great, look different, are more resilient and have a rich history. Heirloom plants are varieties that are at least 50 years old and have survived the test of time. They've been around so long because it's easy to save their seeds and many varieties have been handed down from generation to generation. There are hundreds of different types and it's fun to try something new each season.

Many heirloom vegetables come with interesting names and sometimes fascinating stories. Radiator Charlie's Mortgage Lifter tomato is one example. In the 1930s, Radiator Charlie lived at the top of a big hill. In the heat of summer when trucks came up the hill they often needed Charlie's help – he was a good businessman (location, location, location!). Without any plant breeding experience, he crossed four of his favorite big tomatoes and was able to sell the resulting tomatoes for a dollar apiece. He raised $6,000 and paid off his mortgage, and viola! – Radiator Charlie's Mortgage Lifter was born.

Of course there's nothing wrong with modern hybrid selections either. To make a hybrid, plant breeders cross two plants in hopes of creating a variety with the positive attributes of both parents. The upside is that hybrids are usually vigorous growers and have improved pest tolerance; the downside is that saved seeds from hybrid plants may be sterile and will likely revert to one of the weaker parents. They are often bred for commercial growing and may not have the old-fashioned flavor many gardeners relish.

Check out the list below for some of our favorite varieties, both heirloom and hybrid:

Doug's Favorites	Jessica's Favorites
Tomatoes: 'Brandy Boy' 'Stupice' 'Eva Purple Ball' 'Supersonic' 'Sungold' 'Cherokee Purple'	**Tomatoes:** 'Snow White Cherry' 'Matt's Wild Cherry' 'Striped German'
Beets: 'Detroit Dark Red' 'Long Season'	**Beets:** 'Chioggia' 'Golden Detroit'
Lettuce: 'Deer's Tongue' 'Bronze Arrow' 'Optima'	**Lettuce:** 'Spotted Trout' 'Red Oak Leaf' 'Black Seeded Simpson'
Pole Beans: 'Cherokee Trail of Tears' 'Kentucky Wonder' 'Painted Lady'	**Bush Beans:** 'Golden Wax' 'Royal Burgundy'
Bush Beans: 'Provider' 'Contender'	**Swiss Chard:** 'Bright Lights' 'Rhubarb'
Cucumbers: 'Marketmore 76'	**Potatoes:** 'Rose Gold' 'Russian Banana'
Radish: 'Easter Egg'	**Peppers:** 'Matchbox Hot' 'Malika'

Seeds 101 – starting from scratch

There aren't many things more amazing than watching a seed sprout and poke through the soil. It's a birth of sorts, and watching the plant reach fruition is like having kids, without most of the headaches. Unfortunately, our busy lifestyles are making seed starters rare and that's a shame.

Though more and more small local nurseries are dabbling in growing heirloom and other interesting varieties, it can be a challenge to find the more unusual kinds as started plants. Some of the larger mail order catalogs are now selling heirloom transplants, but they can be pricey and difficult to ship. If you are unable to find any of the cultivars we suggest locally, and you aren't interested in paying big bucks to ship started plants, you'll need to grow your own plants from seed. Many of the seed companies we mention in the Friends of the Organic Gardener appendix sell good quality, reasonably priced seed in an astounding variety. That's the first step in starting your own seeds: buying fresh seed from a reputable company.

What many gardeners find most difficult in starting their own seeds is timing it properly. If you start the seeds too early, you'll end up with leggy plants that are difficult to transplant; if you start them too late, you'll have puny weaklings not yet ready for outdoor conditions. Take note of the "days to maturity" listed on the seed packet. This means the total number of days from germination to harvest. You'll also find a "days to germination" number, which is measured from the time you plant the seed until it pokes its head through the soil surface.

Here's how you figure out your best "sow-by" date: start with the day you'd like to begin to harvest the crop and work backwards by subtracting both the "days to maturity" and "days to germination." That is the date you'll want to start the seeds indoors. It does take a bit of experimentation and some knowledge of your hardiness zone, but it's a good general guideline. Keep track of hits and misses from year to year to avoid making the same mistake twice.

To start the seeds you'll need a few things: containers, growing media (usually potting soil), labels and either plastic wrap or a mini-greenhouse. There are other things you may want to invest in that are not necessary, but helpful. These include heating mats (available from sources listed in the Friends appendix), lights (more about these later) and a misting hose nozzle. And of course you'll need the seeds.

Begin by carefully reading the seed packet and noting the planting depth. Some seeds need light to germinate while others require absolute darkness. The packet will also say if any special conditions will need to be satisfied — conditions like pre-soaking the seeds, nicking particularly hard seed coats (scarification), or refrigerating them for a period of time to expose them to an artificial winter (stratification). Be sure to do any conditioning they recommend, since not doing so will greatly reduce, if not eliminate, germination.

Fill your container with a light potting soil meant specifically for seed starting. Some mixes may contain heavy pieces of bark or strong chemical fertilizers – totally not suitable for delicate seedlings. Tamp the container on a flat surface a few times to settle the soil, but try not to compact it. Place the seeds at the recommended spacing or, if no proper spacing is noted, about 4 times the seed's width. Then cover (or don't) to the proper depth with a light coating of the potting mix. No need to press the seeds into the surface because when you water them in, firm contact will follow.

Label each row carefully and include the date the seeds were sown so you can note it easily in your journal. Watering with a mist nozzle is best, but any light drizzle will do. Make sure the first watering is thorough and the soil is never allowed to dry out. Be sure your container has drainage holes and does not remain in any standing water, as this will prevent necessary air from getting to the roots and may possibly rot the seed even before it germinates.

Cover the top of the container with plastic wrap or a mini-greenhouse to keep up the humidity and reduce the need to water constantly, then place it on a heating mat meant specifically for seed starting. Though not necessary, these mats keep the soil warm while allowing the air to stay cool, preventing disease and speeding germination. Again, many of the sources listed in the Friends appendix sell these mats and they can be used for many years; Jess has had hers for almost 8.

As soon as the seedlings begin to emerge it's important to provide them with adequate light. Delaying this can mean pale, elongated seedlings more prone to disease and transplant shock. While you can invest big bucks in a sophisticated grow light system, regular shop light fixtures with fluorescent bulbs work just fine for seed starting. (You'll need the fancy system if you plan on growing orchids or other flowering plants, but if green is all you want, $11 shop lights will do the trick.) Hang the lights from the ceiling with chains so they can be easily raised and lowered as your seedlings grow. They will need to remain about 2 to 4 inches from the seedling tops. Put them on timers so they shine for about 18 to 20 hours per day, providing enough artificial light to stimulate plenty of strong, sturdy growth. If you don't have space for lights, a sunny south facing windowsill will do; just remember to rotate the containers every day to prevent the seedlings from leaning toward one side.

When 50% of the seedlings have emerged, the plastic covering should be removed; otherwise you risk "frying" them – it gets hot under that plastic! Leaving the plastic on too long also promotes a disease called "damping off" that rots the seedlings at soil level, killing entire batches of seedlings very rapidly.

Once the seedlings form their first true leaves (the second pair that emerge) it's time to carefully transplant them into larger containers – use a standard potting mix for this but try to choose one that does not contain chemical fertilizers. Gently separate the individual seedlings, make a hole with a pencil, insert the roots and lightly fill the hole in with soil. The seedlings can be planted fairly deep at this stage; the soil level should be just under the lowermost pair of leaves. Water them in and begin fertilizing weekly with diluted fish or kelp emulsion or compost tea (for the recipe see the Quick Tips in Chapter 3).

About 3 weeks before you are ready to plant your babies outdoors, you'll need to begin the acclimatization process. You can't just plunk them into the ground; they need some time to adjust to their new environment. Start by placing them in a shaded area outdoors every afternoon for a few hours, then move them back inside. Gradually increase the amount of time they are outside and increase the amount of sunlight they receive as well. Over the course of two weeks you can begin to leave them outdoors at night if no frost is expected. Keep them covered by a light bed sheet or a row cover (see the Glossary) at night for a bit of extra protection. Eventually the sheet will come off and the plants will be fully acclimatized. Skipping this process means certain death for tender seedlings – take your time with it and do it right. What a shame it would be for all your TLC to go to waste!

Now it's time to nestle your newborns into the warm spring soil and keep your fingers crossed for a good season.

Doug

Veggie Relationships – interplanting and combinations

There are good reasons to mix things up in the garden. Instead of planting a whole row or bed of one crop, consider a technique called *interplanting*. This method in and of itself prevents many pests and diseases because we are enabling our plants to profit from one another. One classic version of this technique dates back centuries: it's called a Three Sisters Garden. Native Americans planted corn, pole beans and squash in the same area. The corn offered support for the pole beans, while the squash acted as a living mulch, shading the soil and preventing excess evaporation. As an added bonus, the beans provided nitrogen to their "sisters" by taking it from the air and converting it into a form that is usable by plants (this trait is unique to plants in the bean and pea family).

Another example of interplanting is placing crops that enjoy shadier locations (like lettuce and other greens) underneath taller full-sun plants (like tomatoes and eggplants). The under-story plant helps suppress weeds while the canopy provides much needed shade. You can also interplant to help deter pests. Try planting dill seedlings between your radishes; they'll help drive away flea beetles. See the Quick Tips section of this chapter for more suggestions on interplanting.

Planting certain crops together can result in a symbiotic relationship. We've dedicated an entire chapter to one of these relationships – the connection between the garden and beneficial insects (Chapter 4). These bugs prey upon pest insects and help pollinate our plants. They are the good guys of the garden and they are drawn here by the presence of certain plants. For more about beneficials and their importance to the organic vegetable garden, we suggest you refer back to that chapter.

Feed the Veggies, Feel the Love – fertilization

Every plant needs the same nutrients, just in different amounts. The three nutrients our plants use the most – nitrogen, phosphorus and potassium – are called the primary macronutrients. If you look at any container of fertilizer you'll see three numbers on the label. These numbers represent the percentage of nitrogen, phosphorus and potassium in that bag: that's the N-P-K ratio. Each of these nutrients performs different functions within a plant. Understanding what each nutrient does will go a long way toward improving your vegetable garden's health.

In a nutshell:

- *nitrogen* makes green
- *phosphorus* makes roots and fruits
- *potassium* improves vigor and hardiness.

Crops grown only for their foliage (lettuce, chard, greens, kale, etc.), use a lot of nitrogen. Plants that develop a fruit (tomatoes, eggplants, peppers, etc.) use a lot of phosphorus and potassium. And root crops (beets, potatoes, onions, carrots, etc.) tend to feed heavily on phosphorus. However, *all* garden plants will grow well in good, balanced organic soil. If you've done your job and prepared the soil with a lot of quality organic matter, there's little to worry about. Those nutrients are already present and ready to work for you.

We realize that sometimes the soil falls short, either because you weren't able to add organic matter or you are still working on building your soil. In this situation, a little organic granular fertilizer aimed at specific needs can help provide a needed boost. The following chart lists these fertilizers (all are derived from naturally occurring products) and what they will provide your plants.

Fertilizer	N-P-K Ratio	Comments
Cottonseed meal	6-1-1	An excellent source of slow release nitrogen for greens like lettuce, spinach and chard.
Bone meal	1-13-0	Also contains high amounts of calcium and because of its mild formulation it's perfect for helping seedlings get established.
Feather meal	12-0-0	Great for heavy nitrogen feeders like corn.
Sulfate of potash	0-0-22	Also contains magnesium. It's great for roses and other tender plants.
Alfalfa meal	3-2-2	Perfect all-round choice for the garden. Because it's a fermented product there are millions of microbes present to help invigorate your soil.
Corn gluten meal	10-0-0	Not only does it provide nitrogen, but it also suppresses seed germination. This makes it perfect for lawns and perennial beds as well. Don't use it anywhere you plan to sow seeds.

Respectful Care – maintaining the vegetable garden

Mulching – Mulching is an important chore in any garden, but it is *crucial* in the vegetable garden. Mulch keeps the soil constantly moist, maintains a steady soil temperature, keeps weeding to a minimum, and will add nutrients to the dirt when decomposed. There is a wide variety of material to use. Newspaper is a great choice because it stays moist, will biodegrade and is easy to come by. To mulch with newspaper, lay down about 10 sheets, then take the hose to it (this will prevent it from migrating over to the neighbor's yard when the wind blows). Cover it with a light mulch like straw or grass clippings. If you really want great multi-purpose mulch try compost, leaf mold or mushroom manure. See the mulch chart in Chapter 3 to learn about more choices as well as proper mulching technique.

Support – Just like gardeners at the end of a hard day, many vegetables need support. Whether you use staking, trellising or caging, this support is essential for keeping fruit off the ground, preventing soil-borne disease and maximizing growing space. Stakes come in all shapes and sizes, but a 6-foot-tall 1" x 1" is the standard tomato stake. We prefer stakes made from untreated hardwoods like locust, redwood or cedar; they are good-looking and naturally rot-resistant. Hammer in the stakes at planting time to avoid disturbing the plant's root system and be sure to tie the plants every 8 to 10 inches. You can use any soft twine as a fastener. Our favorite trellises (for cukes, peas and beans) include bamboo lattices, a net made from jute or hemp twine, and tee-pees made from branches and grapevines. In the Quick Tips section we've got a great idea for caging those rowdy tomatoes.

Water – Since water is a precious resource, it's very important to use it wisely and only when necessary. Most plants need an average of 1 inch of water per week – that's from either Mother Nature or the end of your hose. To help reduce water needs and prevent runoff, vegetables should always be planted within a shallow depression. That way, every time it rains water is caught and sent right to the base of the plant. Watering should be done in the early morning. This allows the plants to drink heartily and offers plants susceptible to fungal diseases a chance to dry out before nightfall. It also prevents water from being lost to midday evaporation.

Your best bet for effective irrigation is a drip system. Special soaker hoses are laid in the root zone and water slowly leaches out to keep the plants evenly watered. Most systems work on a timer. If such a system is out of your budget, then water manually with the hose. Ideally you should water only the soil surface, keeping the foliage dry (you'll prevent a lot of bacterial and fungal diseases this way). This means that overhead sprinklers are not the wisest choice, but we know they are sometimes easiest.

Whimsy – Whimsy is a wonderful thing to have anywhere in the landscape, and there are no rules in the vegetable garden. That's where scarecrows, whirligigs, windmills and even the occasional happy gnome all feel at home. Be sure to have a place to sit and enjoy what you've created!

A Plot for All Seasons – the 5-cycle crop rotation system

The single most important practice in the vegetable garden is crop rotation. This simply means never planting the same family of plants in the same place from year to year. Rotating crops is important for many reasons. As we discussed before, plants take different nutrients out of the soil, and by changing the plot each season, the soil gets a break and can be replenished. Another advantage is that over-wintering pests will emerge in the spring and find their host plants absent; and soil-borne diseases, like blight and fungus, will be suppressed. Crop rotation will benefit even the smallest garden. You don't have to move your zucchini a half-acre away, just a few feet will suffice. Of course the farther you can move them, the better.

There are 5 different groups of plants for the vegetable garden:

- *fruit and flower producers* (tomato, pepper, eggplant, tomatillo, broccoli, cauliflower)
- *melons* (cucumber, cantaloupe, watermelon, squash, zucchini, pumpkin)
- *root crops* (carrot, onion, garlic, radish, beet, potato)
- *legumes* (peas and beans)
- *green crops* (cabbage, kale, lettuce, chard, greens)

For this rotation system to be successful, you'll need to keep track of what you plant in each area of the garden. A simple hand-drawn plot plan will do fine. Wait a minimum of three years to plant a member of the same family in that area again. This is usually enough time to flush any problems out of the soil and reestablish nutrient levels.

Better with Birds – attracting our feathered friends to the garden

No organic vegetable garden is complete without the presence of avian workers. Birds eat loads of pest insects, and their presence endows the gardener with both entertainment and a sense of serenity.

Attracting birds to the garden requires creating a habitat that provides three basic needs: food, shelter and water. The food is easy enough, especially if you've got cabbage worms or Japanese beetles! You can also strategically place a feeder in the garden and load it with favorite seed. A birdbath filled frequently with fresh water will keep the birds happily working for you. Moving water, like a fountain, is an even greater draw.

The most important element of the three is shelter. Evergreen shrubs offer a place for birds to rest before coming to the feeder, as well as providing protection from predators. Plant a few small conifers or hollies (whose berries are another food source) around the yard. Often, a feeder will be sited too far from shelter and will be ignored because of the lack of a "staging area."

Building a vegetable garden brings the most tangible rewards a gardener can ask for. You will be blessed with not only the literal fruits of your labor, but also beauty and peace of mind. The knowledge that your food was grown without the use of harmful chemicals is so satisfying. Did you know that the average vegetable travels 2,500 miles from field to table? By growing your own you will know what "fresh" really tastes like!

Doug Tells All *about the finer points of physical labor*

In an annual spring pilgrimage I march out to my vegetable garden, shovel and fork in hand. I've been cultivating these raised beds for years. They are soft and accept the tools with ease. Even though I own a rototiller, it sits idle in the garage. Each season I have the company of a red-bellied woodpecker calling for a mate. As I plunge the fork into the soil, the heel of my boot sends it easily down to sub-soil, revealing plump brown worms who worked all spring to ready the soil for me. Each day I turn over as many beds I can, looking at my rotation plan for guidance. If it's been a season since the soil has been amended, I'll add something nutritious like compost or manure.

The beds for peas, lettuce and radish get turned first. After each has been thoroughly dug, I spread the amendment on top and gently work it into the top few inches of soil. In rows where I plant seeds I also sprinkle an organic granular fertilizer, getting the seeds off to a good start. Transplant holes get an extra shovelful of homemade compost.

Working the soil by hand is not as tough as it sounds and it's rewarding, both mentally and physically. In my opinion, there's really no other way to prepare the soil properly and maintain soil structure. It offers you an up-close look at what each bed is made of – which are the richest and which need work. But it's the time outside with woodpeckers and worms that makes it so worthwhile.

Jess Tells All *about her farm*

When my husband and I bought Muddy Paws Farm four years ago, there was no garden to speak of – unless you count the "wildflower" garden (which was basically a big patch of weeds). I knew in my mind what kind of garden I wanted: the kind that did not consist of row upon row of plants lined up like soldiers. I wanted a garden with pizzazz and funk. I wanted a place to show off my love of interesting combinations and wow my visitors with unusual varieties of vegetables and fun cutting flowers. It took two years, but now I've got just that.

My garden began with my 87-year-old neighbor kindly hitching his plow to the back of his '54 Ford tractor and discing the soil. I didn't kill any weeds first, we just plowed them under. Then we broke out the rototiller, going over the garden again and again until all the lumps were smoothed. I added several truckloads of aged horse manure (from a different neighbor) and another truckload of commercial compost. Then I began to shovel...and shovel, and shovel. I artfully carved paths out by hand and piled all the soil I removed into my growing beds. The beds were raked smooth and the paths were covered with landscape fabric topped with hay (from yet another dear neighbor). Then I began to plant.

The first season is always a learning process in any new garden: the Swiss chard was supreme, the radishes weren't (darned flea beetles!). In my round central bed I planted every variety of herb I could get my hands on, with the full intent of never harvesting them. I put them there for their flowers; I wanted the beneficial insects and pollinators. I planted celosia, sunflowers, Cosmos and amaranth between the tomatoes and eggplants. The beds were all edged in sweet alyssum and gomphrena. How lovely deep green lettuce looks with the bright pink of Zinnias and the deep blue of bachelor's buttons!

My favorite veggie–flower combinations include rhubarb chard with red French sorrel and red celosia; dark purple eggplants with hot pink Cosmos; and purple and green cabbages mixed with blue Salvia.

QUICK TIPS

✂ PLANTING ✂

Horizontal tomatoes

Planting tomatoes horizontally will produce more robust plants. Strip all but the top leaves off the plant, turn it on its side and bury it in a short trench. The stem will sprout lots of roots that are close to the surface of the soil so they stay warm and can better absorb nutrients. If you stake, put the stake in at planting time, otherwise you might drive that stake right through the buried stem.

Space saver

Try planting radishes and carrot seed together. The radishes will be ready to harvest in about a month and will aerate the soil as they are pulled, leaving room for the carrots to take over.

Succession cukes

Plant a second crop of cucumbers a couple of weeks after the first. They will be planted off the cycle of the cucumber beetle and will be more likely to survive.

Extending your lettuce harvest

Sow lettuce seeds every couple of weeks throughout the season to keep the fresh greens coming.

Success with corn

Plant corn in blocks as opposed to rows. The plant is wind-pollinated; more ears will be produced if corn is sown in blocks of at least 4 rows by 4 rows.

Flying saucers

For kids, there's no veggie more fun than flying saucers. Patty pan, or scallopini, squash are easy to grow and fun to eat. They can be picked as small as an inch in diameter or as large as a softball. They are great stuffed with beans and rice or sliced for the grill.

Getting your "ducks" in a row
To plant the straightest rows, run a string from one side to the other and plant along the line.

Herbs
Plant plenty of herbs in your vegetable garden. Their flowers will lure pollinators and you'll be more likely to harvest and use them if they are prominently placed.

❧ TROUBLE ❧

Rotten seeds
Do not buy seeds that have been treated with fungicides. Applied to prevent the seeds from rotting, these fungicides are not organic and they have no place in the organic garden. You'll prevent seed rot organically by planting when the soil has properly warmed and by timing your sowings appropriately.

Blossom end rot
Sunken, black soft spots on the base of your tomatoes and peppers are a sure sign of blossom end rot. Though not a disease, it's often mistaken for one. Blossom end rot is a result of calcium deficiency. This doesn't necessarily mean there is no calcium in your soil; what it does mean is that your plants may not be able to get it. Calcium comes into a plant when it uptakes water, so if your garden has gone through a dry spell, or you aren't watering consistently, your plants can't get enough calcium. Blossom end rot is solved by irrigating regularly.

✂ SEED SAVING ✂

Next year's beans

Beans are one of the easiest plants to save seed from. When the pods are swollen and dried brown, the seed is ready to harvest.

'maters

To save tomato seeds, pick a ripe fruit and squeeze out some of the seeds with their accompanying slime. Let the seeds soak overnight in a glass of water then drain, rinse and add new water. Do this for three days in a row to allow the slime to ferment off. Then spread the seeds on a paper towel to dry. After a week, pack them into envelopes, label them and put them in an airtight container in the fridge.

✂ FOR THE CITY GARDENER ✂

Container choices

If there's no more room in the garden for tomatoes, try a few plants in containers. Choose varieties that are bred to grow in pots (they are often called patio or bush tomatoes). Use the biggest container possible and be sure to water and fertilize throughout the season.

Patio containers

In city gardens with limited space, a raised bed can be constructed using 1" x 12" boards. This box (usually constructed of untreated lumber) can be placed on concrete and filled with a mixture of compost, soil and leaf mold.

✂ PEST DETERRENTS ✂

Cabbage loopers

Cover cole crops like cabbage and broccoli with floating row covers at planting time (see the source appendix for suppliers). The row cover prevents cabbage butterflies from laying eggs on them. The larvae of these small white butterflies are green worms called cabbage loopers.

Cutworms

To deter the dreaded cutworm (these little critters chop off stalks of plants like a lumberjack), insert a toothpick vertically on either side of the stem of newly planted seedlings. The worm is unable to circle the plant and is foiled. Collars of toilet paper tubes cut to 1 inch high work too.

Tomato hornworm

Never kill a tomato hornworm that has little white eggs on its back. These are the eggs of a parasitic wasp and as soon as they hatch the larvae will burrow into the hornworm, killing it. In about a week they emerge from their host as adults in search of another hornworm.

Deer and other mammals

There is a motion-activated sprinkler called The Scarecrow. It's not used to water the garden, but to deter the deer. We've heard lots of folks have had success using it. Just put it in the veggie garden, connect it to the hose and set up the video camera! It also works for intruding dogs and cats.

✄ HARVESTING, STORING AND PRESERVING ✄

Picking right

Always harvest your veggies in the morning. This is when their moisture content is at its highest and they will store longer. Cut tomatoes, peppers, cukes and other fruits off the plants instead of pulling. That way you won't risk tearing the stem.

Zucchini woes

Have some extra zucchini? Shred it in the food processor then let it sit in a colander for an hour to drain off the excess water. Pack it into freezer bags for baking zucchini bread all winter. Another way to use up that excess is to get a lovely basket, fill it with zucchini, put it on the neighbor's porch, ring the bell and run.

Freezing method

Freeze freshly picked veggies as soon as possible; this prevents their natural sugars from turning to starch. Most veggies can be frozen after blanching them in boiling water for 3 minutes. Follow the blanching with a prompt cold-water bath, then drain and pack into freezer bags. This method works for beans, peas, corn, broccoli, cauliflower, shredded cabbage and greens.

✄ DESIGN WITH FINESSE ✄

Paths

When designing your garden, consider grass paths instead of something like gravel or woodchips. There's nothing better than barefoot walks through the vegetable garden, picking summer tomatoes.

Really raised beds

Feel energetic? Build a few 3-foot-high raised beds out of concrete block. No more bending over to weed (except now the deer don't have to bend down for lunch either!).

Color your world

We love to see unusually colored vegetables planted with traditional varieties. Contact some of the suppliers in the source appendix for purple broccoli, pink chard, yellow beets and purple beans. These heirloom choices will draw attention and taste fabulous.

Cutting flowers

The veggie garden is an ideal place to plant flowers for cutting – for some reason you'll feel less guilty about lopping off their heads! It will be easy to pick a bouquet while you're harvesting other goodies and they will be readily accessible. Try Zinnias, Cosmos, amaranth, snapdragons and other annuals. You can start them from seed either indoors or directly in the garden.

✈ RECYCLE AND REUSE ✈

Milk jugs reincarnated

Make your own cloches (see Glossary) by cutting the bottoms out of plastic milk jugs. Place one jug over each broccoli, cabbage or lettuce transplant to keep them warm during unpredictable early spring weather. Be sure to remove them once daytime temperatures reach the 70s, to prevent foliage burn.

Plant ties

Tear your old bedsheets and pantyhose into strips and use them to tie up your tomatoes. They can be reused for many years.

ADVANCED QUICK TIPS

✈ SEASON EXTENDERS ✈

Winter gardening

An early fall sowing of cool season greens like kale, collards, chard and lettuce can be harvested through most of the winter months with a little extra protection. Make 18-inch-high semicircles of heavy gauge wire to form hoops over the rows. Cover this "tunnel" with heavyweight row cover or clear plastic sheeting. Weigh down the edges with soil or rocks and simply lift to harvest. Make sure to put your tunnels up before a hard frost to help capture heat and keep the soil temperatures warm. Heavily mulching the soil with straw, hay or grass clippings will help as well. There's nothing better than bragging to other gardeners about harvesting in January!

Storing root crops

Extending the storage life of root crops like carrots and beets is easy. After harvesting, remove the greens and brush off the excess soil. Pack them in wooden crates filled with damp sand and place the crates in a cool basement or root cellar. Be sure the roots aren't in contact with each other; this ensures that should one go "bad," the rest of the batch will not be affected.

Getting early tomatoes

Use breathable black landscape fabric (available at most garden centers) under tomatoes. Prepare the soil normally, then lay the fabric over the dirt as early in the season as possible. It helps warm up the planting area – tomatoes love hot soil. Make a hole in the fabric at planting time, and plant right through it; then cover the fabric with straw for a more attractive appearance.

Late tomatoes

Although most gardeners long for the first tomato of the season, the last can be just as rewarding. During wet summers some plants tend to stop producing at the end of the season. Plant some early maturing varieties about 3 weeks after your normal planting date. They will begin to mature as the earlier crop is dwindling.

Earlier beets

For a jump on the beet season: in late winter, plant some seed in peat pots under grow lights or on a bright windowsill. The beets can then be planted out a bit earlier, pot and all. Eventually the pot just rots away and the beets will be ready to harvest weeks before your neighbors'.

Summer "spinach"

Try growing Malabar or New Zealand spinach in the summer. Although neither is really a spinach, they taste like it and won't bolt in hot weather, enabling you to harvest their greens until frost.

Straight carrots

To ensure perfect carrots, till the planting area to a depth of 18 inches and work in plenty of organic matter. If your soil is rocky, plan on spending some extra time removing any stones from your carrot bed; their presence will cause the roots to bend or branch. For the sweetest taste and softest crunch, pick homegrown carrots when they are as thick as your thumb – any thicker and you risk a pithy center.

Funky veggies

Try something fun in the garden. Grow kohlrabi, winged beans, rutabagas, Jerusalem artichokes, edamame beans, mustard greens and celerac.

Of birds and corn

If marauding birds steal your corn or pea seeds even before they can germinate, build a maze of jute twine over the area as soon as it's planted. Simply randomly insert several 6-inch branches into the soil and wrap the twine around them, creating a grid of twine about 2 inches above the soil surface. The birds won't risk getting tangled and at the end of the season the string can just go onto the compost pile.

✂ VEGGIE SUPPORT ✂

Tomato cages

Tired of those flimsy store-bought tomato cages? Use concrete reinforcement wire to build your own. The 8-inch-square openings make harvesting those beefsteaks a snap. Just cut a piece about 5 feet high and 10 feet long, wrap it into a cylinder and plant in the center.

✂ WATERING ✂

Rain barrels

Rain barrels can be a terrific investment for the organic gardener. Purchase one with a spout at the bottom for easy hose connection. We love old oak wine barrels for this purpose – they look charming and weather well. To deter mosquitoes in your rain barrel, use dunks of the biological insecticide Bt *(Bacillius thuringiensis)*. It won't hurt your plants or you!

Capillary matting

To make watering trays of seedlings much easier, and much less frequent, use capillary matting. This fibrous material is placed under the trays and acts as a wick, absorbing moisture from a reservoir located nearby and transferring it to the plants' roots. Simply place one end of the matting in the reservoir (making sure it's constantly full), be sure the drainage holes in all the containers are in firm contact with the mat, and let your plants water themselves. They will draw in moisture as needed without the risk of "drowning" themselves. See the Friends appendix for sources.

✂ ADVANCED SEED SAVING ✂

Lettuce breeding

Let a couple of lettuce plants go to seed and collect it before it falls off the plant. Choose seed from the last plant to flower, thus preserving that lateness trait. The seeds should be saved in an airtight container and stored in a cool dark place. Mason jars are great choice for storing seed. If you do this over a few seasons, you'll "breed" a lettuce that will withstand longer days and warmer temperatures.

✄ SOIL PREPARATION ✄

Double digging

For real backbreaking work (but worth every trip to the physical therapist) try double digging. The top 18 to 24 inches of soil is dug out and piled to the side of the garden. Use a fork to loosen the subsoil, then add organic matter. Now dig the same sized area right next to the current bed. Use the surface soil being dug from that bed to fill the one you just dug. This goes on until the end of the bed, and the last trench is filled with the first soil that was dug out.

Phosphorus

Because phosphorus helps roots get established and grow, and helps with fruiting and flowering, phosphorus deficiency can have dramatic effects. Not only does phosphorus need to be in the soil, but it needs to be located fairly close to the roots. Unlike some other nutrients that can come into a plant with water, there is a very small area around a plant's roots from which phosphorus can be absorbed. So when your soil test says you need to add phosphorus, you may want to apply it as a side dressing. This means putting it right near the root zone of your plants where it can be easily absorbed – it does not mean that you should add extra. Too much of a good thing can result in burned plants or toxicity.

7

Getting to the Fruit of the Matter
The Home Orchard

In an orchard there should be enough to eat, enough to lay up,
enough to be stolen, and enough to rot on the ground.
- James Boswell

A certain satisfaction comes with eating a fresh apple right off the tree. It's crisp, it's sweet, and best of all, it's safe (if it's grown without chemicals, of course!). Commercially produced fruit is loaded with conventional pesticides and fungicides; sure it looks perfect, but at what cost? And where's that tree-ripened, fresh-picked flavor?

Some folks think it's impossible to grow quality fruit organically, but nothing could be further from the truth. We accept this pleasant challenge and try our best to educate these disbelievers about the realities of the organic home orchard. This is what we know: you can produce your own organic fruit with astounding flavor and beauty by doing three things – choosing the right plants, caring for them properly, and managing diseases and pests before they get out of hand. And when you bite into your first crop of organic fruit you'll be at ease with the knowledge that you're eating something not only homegrown, but chemical-free.

Your first orchard – ensuring its success

Planning an orchard is something not to be taken lightly. Spend time thinking about it and consider what you want to accomplish in growing fruit. Do you want apples for baking or to eat fresh? Do you love peaches, plums, pears or maybe something exotic like the native pawpaw or persimmon? Do you have limited space and the ability to grow only small fruits like blueberries or currants (if so, we've got a special section for you a little later in the chapter)? Start with choosing plants suited to both your needs and your space restrictions.

One of the most therapeutic activities a gardener can do is creating a plan for the next phase of the garden. You usually do this during the off-season, working with graph paper and pencil to make a detailed master plan; nothing fancy, a simple line drawing will suffice. Choosing a place to plant an orchard is like deciding where the pumpkins should be planted in the vegetable garden. It's critical that there be enough space for them to mature – but if you make a mistake with pumpkins you're sorry for a season; blow it with trees and you'll regret it for decades.

Full-sized fruit trees each need up to 30 feet of space. Semi-dwarf and dwarf trees need considerably less; some dwarf varieties can be planted as close as 8 feet apart. Before deciding what kind of trees you will grow, examine the size of your planting area. Always keep the size of the mature tree in mind. It's a common mistake to underestimate how big a full-grown tree will get when you go to plant that little sapling.

Many fruit trees need a *cross-pollinator* – another tree (within the same species) to share pollen and help increase the fruit production of both trees. In fact, some trees won't bear fruit unless there is a cross-pollinator present. Good purveyors of fruit trees will provide you with lists of suggested pollination combos. It's necessary to pay close attention to this since, even within the same type of fruit tree, bloom time varies as does pollen compatibility. When deciding what to plant where, take into account the possible necessity of planting multiple trees. Luckily, if a close neighbor has an orchard and is growing the same types of fruit, you may not need to plant your own pollinator; it may already be there.

Be sure to keep the garden neat and tidy. Dead plant material and other assorted debris are a haven for veggie-eating critters like slugs and earwigs. Keep your tomatoes staked or caged and off the ground; soil-borne blights will find it harder to contact the leaves.

Eye-catching bunches of mixed beets brighten up the garden and taste out of this world. 'Golden,' 'Chioggia' and 'Red Ace' beets are just a few of the many cultivars suited to the organic garden.

Make a place for birds in your landscape by providing shelter, water and food. Sunflowers, black-eyed-Susans, coneflowers, crabapples and many other ornamentals provide both seeds and winter perches for our feathered friends.

Don't forget to have fun with your garden. Use your personality to add a little flair; support local artists and find what makes you smile.

A 3-bin compost system makes for smooth sailing. Doug describes this, his favorite composting system, in Chapter 3 and gives plenty of hints for creating your own "black gold."

No one said rows have to be uniform. Sometimes doing something as simple as planting your lettuce on the bias or inter-planting different varieties can spice things up a bit. 'Hyper Red Ruffle,' 'Deer's Tongue,' 'Spotted Trout,' 'Red Oakleaf' and 'Black Seeded Simpson' are easy to start from seed, and young shoots can be harvested for weeks.

Ladybugs are probably the most familiar beneficial insect. The adults and larvae feed on soft-bodied insects like aphids, scale and mealybugs. Bring them to your garden by planting plenty of herbs and other plants that have clusters of small flowers.

When designing the garden, plan for some structure and winter interest. Blooming shrubs, ornamental fencing, statuary and walls provide beauty and balance – while evergreens, trees with mottled bark, and plants with berries and pods pique your garden curiosity even when the snow flies.

The vegetable garden does not have to be boring. Select varieties with interesting foliage colors and bright venation, then plant them to compliment each other. Red French sorrel, Greek basil and tri-colored amaranth make fine neighbors for a deep red Celosia.

Chickens and ducks can be great friends of the organic garden. If your local ordinances (and your spouse) allow, keeping a few hens in the yard will provide pest control, fresh eggs, free compost ingredients and plenty of entertainment. Jess recommends reading *Storey's Guide to Raising Chickens* to learn more.

Rain barrels are an ideal way to recycle valuable rain water. From fancy oak to practical plastic, they provide an easy way to keep containers and window boxes from drying out. Just empty the contents into watering cans and sprinkle away.

Frogs and toads eat a huge amount of insect pests – who else is going to eat a slug? Encourage them by building a year-round water feature in the yard, by providing plenty of shady resting places, and by mulching (they love to nestle underneath the mulch on hot sunny days).

Plant plenty of flowers in the vegetable garden to attract beneficial insects and pollinators. They will not only kick the garden up a notch, but they'll keep it healthy and buzzing.

Locate your orchard in an area with full sun and well-drained soil. An open, sunny locale will help prevent fungal issues and a good fertile soil will help the trees fight off diseases and insects. Avoid low areas like the bottom of valleys; frost can collect there and nip the spring buds, severely affecting the quantity of fruit produced in the event of a late frost.

Once your orchard has found a home, move on to variety selection. Shop carefully and pay attention to all the details; they include mature size, disease and pest resistance (especially important in organic production), ripening dates, cross-pollination compatibility and, of course, taste and texture. To help in the selection process, we've listed our favorite sources for edible fruits in the Friends appendix. Below you'll find a chart listing some of our personal favorites.

Doug's favorites	Jessica's favorites
Apples: 'Jon-A-Red' 'Red Rome' 'Goldrush' 'Red Fuji'	**Apples:** 'Liberty' 'Northern Spy' 'Yellow Transparent' 'Gravenstein'
Peaches: 'Early White Giant Peach' 'Hale Haven Dwarf' 'Golden Jubilee'	**Peaches:** 'Avalon Pride' 'New Haven' 'Sweet Bagel'
Raspberries: 'Heritage Red Everbearing' 'Latham Red' 'Fall Gold'	**Raspberries:** 'Amity'
Blackberries: 'Triple Crown Thornless'	**Apricot:** 'Harglow' 'Puget Gold'
Pears: 'Bartlett' 'Red Sensation'	**Pears:** 'Honey Sweet' 'Harrow Delight'
Pawpaw: 'Pennsylvania Golden' 'Sunflower'	**Blueberries:** 'Bluecrop' 'Patriot' 'Jersey' 'Brigitta'

Plums: 'Methley' 'Early Golden'	**Plums:** 'Persian Green' 'Seneca' 'Early Laxton'
Cherries: 'Hartland' 'Black Gold' 'Rainier'	**Persimmon:** 'Hachiya'
Grapes: 'Claret' 'Glenora' 'Concord Seedless'	**Kiwi:** 'Saanichton' 'Exbury'
Strawberries: 'Earlyglow' 'Tri Star' 'Seascape'	**Quince:** 'Havran'

Home Sweet Home – planting techniques made easy

No matter what varieties you choose, you'll have to decide how you'd like to purchase them – and we don't mean whether you'll pay with cash or credit. Trees can be purchased one of three ways: bare root, potted in a container, or balled and burlapped.

Bare root trees are most often offered in catalogs and are usually one- to three-year-old saplings shipped without any soil covering their roots (hence the name bare root). They are stored and shipped in a dormant state, so you can only purchase them for late winter or early spring planting. When the tree arrives, unwrap it and place the roots in tepid water for a few hours before planting. It might seem scary to get a tree with no soil, but it's a common practice and one we recommend – especially when you're looking for interesting or uncommon varieties.

Potted trees work almost as well and often can be bought locally; shipping is understandably a problem when mailing a 45-pound tree across the country. The most common problem with potted trees is their tendency to be pot-bound. With root systems circling within the pot or growing out the bottom drainage holes, these trees will suffer a bit of transplant shock and will need some TLC. A pot-bound tree needs to have its roots loosened, cut or unwrapped before planting – it sounds like a brutal process, but it is absolutely essential for encouraging those roots to spread out into the existing soil.

Balled and burlapped trees are dug from the growing field with a special tractor implement. The root system and its surrounding soil are wrapped in burlap and often enclosed in a wire cage. If the root ball is not disturbed during planting the success rate is high, but if the ball is cracked or planted too deeply there could be problems. The wire cage is always removed before planting (you will need to cut it off with a sturdy pair of wire cutters) and the burlap is removed only from the area immediately surrounding the trunk. The trick is to dislodge all this stuff after the tree is positioned in the planting hole; otherwise the fragile ball of soil may fracture.

No matter how you purchase your trees, early spring is the best time to get digging. Late fall is another option, but you may have a hard time finding fruit trees then, especially bare root ones.

A word to the wise: When planting your fruit trees, don't make the mistake of carving out a planting hole from clay and then filling it with compost or another soil amendment. The roots of the tree will stay in the nice cozy compost hole and continue to circle around; and they will eventually strangle the tree. It's better to loosen an area 2 to 3 times wider than the root ball (but no deeper) and backfill the tree with the existing soil. Really, we are honestly saying NOT to add any organic matter! By not amending the soil, the roots are encouraged to stretch out in search of nutrients and water. It also persuades them to quickly acclimate to the soil they will be spending the rest of their life in. Basically, you aren't giving them a choice – spread your roots as quickly as possible. You'll find this makes for an amazingly self-sufficient adult tree (we're talking any tree here, not just fruit bearers).

Once the tree is planted it will need to be watered in. Jess turns her hose on a trickle and places it at the base of the tree for several hours. This helps settle the soil and ensures a thorough, penetrating watering. Water your new tree regularly throughout its first year in the garden. At the end of a full year, the roots have grown sufficiently to provide the tree with all the water and nutrients it needs. With the exception of periods of extreme drought, no more watering is required, nor is any supplemental fertilizer.

Next, the saplings should be mulched. Compost is an effective tool for the job, as is shredded bark or chopped leaves. Never let the mulch touch the bark of the tree, since any contact may cause disease problems and offer a warm hiding place for bark nibbling rodents – mice are notorious for feeding on the bark of fruit trees during the winter, leaving them girdled and headed for an untimely death. Check out this chapter's Quick Tips section for more ideas on deterring deer and rabbits in the orchard.

The Little Things – fruit for space-deprived gardeners

If a full-out orchard is not really an option for you, keep in mind that fruit trees come in many sizes and can be grown in the ornamental landscape as well. Instead of putting in another dogwood or maple, try planting a dwarf cherry or an old-fashioned quince. Even large containers can be home to small fruit trees, as long as the plants are properly watered and fertilized.

A technique called *espalier*, which dates back thousands of years, is a great way to grow full-sized fruit in small spaces. By training a young plant to grow against a wall or along a wire trellis you save space, but also create an interesting ornamental effect. It's basically a two-dimensional tree. You can purchase them already trained from specialty nurseries or you can learn about espalier in many detailed fruit-growing manuals.

Gardeners with limited space will find smaller fruits ideal. Crops like blueberries, huckleberries, currants, gooseberries and strawberries are perfect for gardens of all sizes. Raspberries and blackberries need room to ramble, but they are quick growing and heavy bearing and are worth making room for. For more about growing small fruits see the Quick Tips section.

The Buzz on Bees – all about pollination

With the decline of European honeybee populations, in addition to the drop in native bee numbers, many orchards are finding themselves in need of some pollination help. Large-scale fruit growing operations rent hives from beekeepers during bloom season; it ensures proper pollination and results in larger fruit (the more ovaries fertilized, the heftier the fruit). You can improve fruit set in your own orchard by placing a honeybee hive in the corner of the orchard. Many local apiarists actively seek out homes for their hives and you may get some honey out of the deal too. Beekeepers love to teach others about their art and soon enough you may find yourself decked out in a netted pith helmet and toting a bee smoker.

Boosting native bee populations will also improve the orchard's production. Mason bees are perfect pollinators. They are gentle and nest in small holes in wood. They do not excavate wood; instead, they look for any existing, properly sized holes. Some gardeners put up nesting blocks made of pine or fir drilled with 1/4- and 3/8-inch holes about 3 to 6 inches deep and spaced about 1/2 inch apart. Eventually the bees will find the block and start to use it as a nesting site, pollinating your trees as rent. Chapter 4's Quick Tips section has more great ideas for increasing native bee numbers and purchasing adult mason bees.

Pruning Like You Mean It

Entire books have been written about proper pruning techniques for fruit trees, and even then many gardeners still need help. In our opinion, the best way to learn is by asking someone who's an expert or taking a pruning class at the local nursery, garden center or orchard. No doubt, learning pruning through a hands-on workshop is the best way to go. Because of this, instead of detailing specific pruning methods, let's talk about why pruning is so important.

Pruning is done to regulate growth and to improve the quality and size of the fruit. Most fruit tree pruning is performed annually in late winter, when the plant is dormant and its structure is easily seen. Fruit trees are also pruned to control size and help keep the picking easy. You may have noted that in commercial orchards the branches are thick but close enough to the ground so that only a small ladder is needed to pick all the fruit – a useful strategy in home orchards as well.

The first few years of a fruit tree's care are critical to future performance. Any cuts you make now will determine the permanent framework of the tree as it matures. The goal is to produce strong enough branches to support lots of sweet fruit and to create a tree with plenty of room for flowers and fruits to fully develop. Plenty of air circulation to help prevent disease is an added bonus of proper pruning. Take the time to learn how to do it right and you will not be disappointed; it is time and money well spent.

Dealing with the Bad Guys – protecting your fruit from harm

For most fruit trees there are two potential problems: insect pests and fungal diseases. Both are best handled by employing proper preventive measures and developing a good spray regimen (which we'll detail a bit later). The easiest preventive measure to employ is the practice of maintaining a "clean" orchard. Pick up any dropped fruit and remove any old fruit still hanging on the trees at the end of the season. Since many common fruit pests exit from dropped fruit to over-winter in the soil, collecting and discarding unusable fruit helps reduce their population. And fungal diseases will easily survive the winter as spores clinging to any remaining fruit and leaves (we call any shriveled-up, moldy fruits still clinging to the tree "mummies") – so climbing a ladder to pluck off the mummies at season's end will reduce the number of spores present the following spring. Other, more specific, preventive measures are detailed below where we discuss several common pest and disease issues in turn.

Common fruit pests

Apple maggots can cause havoc in even the smallest of orchards. Female flies lay eggs just under the skin of the apple. As the larvae (the maggots) hatch, they tunnel through the fruit. In a few weeks the maggots will leave the fruit, drop to the ground and burrow in. They will eventually pupate into more adult flies that go on to produce yet another generation. Though most common on apples, you'll also occasionally find the maggots feeding on plums, pears and cherries.

The best preventive method is to hang red balls, coated in a non-drying glue on the tree in the middle of June and leave them on until the end of the season – a single sphere for a small dwarf variety and up to 6 spheres for a full-sized specimen. These red balls lure and trap the adult flies, who think they are ripe apples and land to lay their eggs (both the balls and the glue are found in many of the sources listed in the Friends appendix).

Codling moths attack apple, pear, peach and quince. Larvae spend the winter in cocoons hidden under bark, leaf litter or other debris. In spring they pupate, take flight, mate and lay eggs on the fruit or leaves. A few weeks later the newly hatched larvae feed in channels they create inside the fruit and head for the core where they consume the seeds. They will then leave the fruit through a separate exit hole and start the cycle again – many times producing two generations in a season.

The best preventive method is to use pheromone traps to lure and capture the adults. These traps are hung in the trees a couple weeks before bud break and will need to be replaced in July to control the second hatch. Two traps per full-sized tree will suffice. For more information about pheromone traps, check out the book's final chapter on natural pest management.

The Plum curculio plagues its namesake, but will also attack nectarines, peaches, cherries, apricots, pears, quince and sometimes blueberries. The adult weevil survives the winter in leaf litter, emerging at bloom time and feeding on any developing fruit. The adults leave tell tale crescent-shaped scars as they eat; they then go on to lay eggs under the skin of the fruit. A week later the newly hatched larvae bore through the fruit and feed for several weeks. The larvae then drop to the ground, burrow, pupate, and emerge as adults in late summer. These adults feed for the remainder of the season before finding a home for the winter.

Plum curculio used to be an especially difficult pest to prevent, but recently developed products based on *kaolin clay* work wonders. Sprayed on the fruit as a liquid, it then dries to form a thin, powdery barrier around the fruit, repelling the adults and preventing them from laying their eggs (they don't like the feeling of the clay particles clinging to their body). The clay is edible and is commonly found in toothpaste and Kaopectate, though the fruit should still be washed before eating. Begin spraying at petal drop and continue to do so every 7 to 10 days for about 8 applications (some folks prefer to do it for the entire season, since it helps deter other pests as well). Trees look a little funny coated in the white spray, but if the plum curculio is a problem in your orchard, it's well worth it. Kaolin clay products also help deter apple maggots and codling moths too – you'll note that it's an important step in the organic care regimen we detail later.

Peach tree borers feed under the bark of trees and attack peaches, plums, cherries, nectarines, apricots and plums. Adult moths lay eggs on the bark in mid to late summer. The larvae hatch and burrow under the bark, tunneling between the inner bark and the sap wood. The larvae over-winter then emerge as adults early the following summer. They then go on to mate and lay up to 500 eggs. Borers can kill young trees when the trunks are girdled by their feeding. Eventually the bark will peel off the affected areas; this weakens the whole tree leaving it susceptible to other insects and diseases.

Preventive methods for peach tree borers include the promotion of beneficial insects such as lacewings and spiders, which naturally prey on the pest. You can also use pheromone traps to capture and monitor the adults. Promising research is also pointing to the effectiveness of a species of beneficial nematode, *Steinernema carpocapsae*, "injected" into the hole of the borer with a needle-less syringe (sources for the nematodes are listed in the Friend's appendix). If you find the entrance holes in fall, indicated by the presence of the insect's excrement or sap weeping from the hole, you can also use a piece of straightened wire or a paperclip to "worm" the tree. Push the wire into the hole as far as it will go to squash the borer.

Common Fruit Diseases

The key to dramatically reducing the number of fungal and bacterial diseases in your orchard is threefold:

- Keep a "clean" orchard. This is essential. Collect fallen fruit and leaves and disinfect your pruners and saws between trees.

- Properly prune your trees. This radically reduces diseases by providing proper air circulation. This also helps fruit to dry off faster after rain, and since many fungal issues crop up in wet conditions, this simple practice can make a real difference. Keep any dead or infected wood out of the tree as well.

- Choose disease-resistant varieties. This is the single most important thing you can do to reduce diseases. Why plant a variety prone to developing problems when there are so many other delicious, trouble-free choices?

Brown rot most commonly attacks peaches, apricots, nectarines and plums. The disease appears as brown, soft, fuzzy cankers on ripening fruit, but it can also turn blossoms to mush before they are even pollinated. It is most common during wet, rainy seasons, but the spores are wind borne, so an infection can occur anytime. The spores of brown rot spend winters on twigs or infected fruit; again, a clean orchard is a must. Remove infected fruit and dispose of them in the garbage, not in the compost pile.

Bacterial spot begins 4 to 5 weeks after petal fall as small, scattered, sunken brown pits on peaches, apricots, nectarines, and plums. You'll also find dark spots on the leaves that are more severe towards the leaf tip. Often the lesions are surrounded by paler colored sections and are accompanied by star-shaped surface cracks.

Black rot on grapes begins as tiny, reddish brown spots on leaves. Infected fruits develop a light spot that grows and darkens until entire grape is infected. The grape will then dry, shrivel, and turn black. It can affect entire clusters of grapes or individual fruits.

Botrytis on strawberries, raspberries, grapes, kiwis, and stone fruit appears as fuzzy brown or grey mold and spreads rapidly, especially in wet conditions. Prune away excess grape foliage as the fruits begin to develop and keep strawberry plants well spaced and mulch to keep the fruits off the ground. Kiwis should hang freely beneath the vines to improve air circulation, and stone fruits will need to be appropriately pruned.

Apple scab appears as brown and black spots on leaves and makes the fruit skin look "rough" and mottled. Many times scab causes the fruit to drop early. The disease over-winters on both the dropped leaves and the fallen fruit. There are many resistant varieties on the market, including 'Liberty,' 'Honeycrisp' and 'Freedom.'

Flyspeck fungus arrives on apples when nights are warm and the weather is humid. It looks like tiny black specks scattered in groups on the skin of apples. Flyspeck does not damage fruit and only mars the skin's surface. Although the apples don't look good, peel them. They will taste just as good as non-infected fruit.

Cedar apple rust develops as reddish-orange spots on leaves. The good news: infection time is relatively short – they can only pick up the spores until just after petal drop. Often the fruit of infected apple trees will fall prematurely. The rust spores spend the winter portion of their lifecycle on junipers and cedars. Be sure to plant one of the many resistant cultivars.

Sooty blotch is an aesthetic issue with apples, just like flyspeck. The fungus prefers warm nights and humid weather to take hold. It appears as patchy, sooty grey areas on the skin of apples and does not affect the interior of the fruit.

There are, of course, other insect pests and diseases that will readily use your fruit trees as host – from scales to locusts, blights to cankers. If you have a different problem from those common ones we list above, please read Chapter 9, which details our simple 6-step approach to organic pest management.

Fruit Protection – developing a good spraying program

Vital to the maintenance of an organic orchard is a consistent and well-timed spray program. In the book's final chapter on pest management we spend a lot of time convincing you *not* to spray unless it's absolutely necessary. For organic fruit production, most folks find a good spray regimen (using only natural, organic products of course) a huge help, albeit not 100% necessary. We're not saying you won't get fruit unless you spray; rather, that by following some good cultural practices (like proper spacing and pruning), using all available preventive measures and applying the right stuff at the right time, you will get grocery store quality fruit (and better!) from your organic garden. That being said, gardeners must still take precautions, even when spraying organic materials. Always spray on windless days, follow all label instructions and always use a respirator and eye protection.

Below, we have detailed a typical spray regimen for most standard and dwarf fruit-bearing trees, separating them into the categories of stone fruits (peaches, plums, apricots, nectarines, cherries) and seed fruits (apples, pears, persimmons). Most of the smaller fruits (strawberries, blueberries, rasp and blackberries) are handled in the Quick Tips section. Of course, home orchardists may choose to grow other less common fruits as well (like citrus, pomegranates, pawpaws, currants and the like) and we encourage you to experiment. This regimen may work for many of these fruits too, but you'll want to do a little investigating first to ensure everything will be effective and reliable for that particular crop.

Lastly, if you'd like more information about any of the organic products we mention below, you'll need to see the product list we provide in Chapter 9. It details each one of them specifically and lets you know exactly how best to use them.

Fruit Care Regimen – season by season

Stone fruits:

Late winter – Prune and apply horticultural oil to smother any over-wintering pests or insect eggs.

Early spring – Hang codling moth pheromone traps before the buds open.

Spring – As soon as the fruit has formed begin spraying an organic fungicide (lime sulfur, *Bacillus subtilis* or a potassium bicarbonate product) at 14 to 21-day intervals to control diseases; when petals drop, spray with kaolin clay every 7 to 10 days for 8 straight applications (or longer) to deter various insect pests.

Summer – Replace codling moth pheromone traps in mid-July; continue regular applications of an organic fungicide; collect damaged fruit as it falls from tree.

Autumn – Examine the bark for the holes created by borers, inject with beneficial nematodes or "worm" the tree as described above; collect all fallen fruit and leaves and discard properly; record in your journal any successes or failures.

Seed fruits:

Late winter – Prune and apply horticultural oil to smother any over-wintering pests or insect eggs.

Early spring – Hang codling moth pheromone traps before the buds open.

Spring – As soon as the fruit has formed begin spraying an organic fungicide (lime sulfur, *Bacillus subtilis* or a potassium bicarbonate product) at 14 to 21-day intervals to control diseases; when petals drop, spray with kaolin clay every 7 to 10 days for 8 straight applications (or longer) to deter various insect pests.

Summer – In mid-June hang red sphere sticky traps in apple trees for apple maggots; replace codling moth pheromone traps in mid-July; continue regular applications of an organic fungicide; collect damaged fruit as it falls from tree.

Autumn – Collect all fallen fruit and leaves and discard properly; record in your journal any successes or failures.

The orchard is a wonderful place to gather, even if your orchard consists of only two peach trees in the backyard. Many memories are made as sweet fruits are enjoyed with family and friends. Whether it's a glass of wine under a grape arbor or a child's first soft ripe peach, growing your own fruit is well worth the effort.

Doug Tells All   *about heartbreak*

"Peaches will break your heart." So says the advice I got from gardening friend Burt Bloom. He was lamenting the cold blasts of spring air that froze the soft pink petals, denying him fruit for a whole year. He chronicled the devastation of brown rot as it took most of his crop just before maturity. The list went on, and he was also one of the guys who told me I could never grow peaches organically.

I took the challenge, knowing what he said couldn't be true. I planted three different peach trees in my new orchard, carved out of an opening in the trees on my 4-acre wooded lot. It was the only area left that might have enough sun to make the trees thrive. These semi-dwarf varieties were perfect for the small space I had, and I planted them on 15-foot centers. I also planted four apple, two pear, and two pawpaw trees.

A 7-foot-high plastic fence was put in place to deter the abundant deer herd patrolling the forest. Occasionally during the winter an ice storm would take part of the fence down and a buck would enjoy rubbing the trees. Each year I would resign myself to the fact that one tree would die, only to be pleasantly surprised by the rejuvenative power these fruit trees possess.

I read everything I could find about organic fruit production and dutifully started the next season by coating the saplings with horticultural oil in late winter. Despite my good intentions, it would be the last time I ever sprayed any of them with anything. Know what? I still get fruit every year – it's not perfect, but it still tastes great.

Seems those peaches are tasty to someone else too. Raccoons are the ones enjoying the harvest each season. They usually beat me to the ripe fruit. So my wife and I end up either picking a few peaches early to ripen indoors, or we're left to find a few on the ground that the raccoons "forgot."

You were right, Burt. Peaches (and raccoons) will break your heart.

Jess Tells All   *about homegrown pleasures*

Gardening on a quarter acre suburban lot did not deter my mother. Of course, back then everyone in our neighborhood had a garden to help feed the family. What everyone did not have was a backyard orchard. My parents planted a peach, nectarine, pear, apricot, plum, two cherries, an apple, three blueberry bushes, two grape vines, black raspberries, a strawberry patch and two filbert trees on that small lot. I guess they saw the practicality of growing edible plants instead of ornamental ones.

I have great memories (and the pictures to back them up) of standing on ladders to harvest peaches as big as my head. All the neighbor kids would help with the picking; they knew they'd get to take some fruit home as payment. I remember my mom drying apple and nectarine slices in our food dehydrator and spreading out puréed fruits to make homemade fruit leather. I remember my father jamming a straightened paperclip into the tiny holes made by the peach tree borers at the base of our tree. And I remember my sister and me being disappointed each year there were no cherries (turns out we never did get any…).

Some of my nicest garden memories involve my neighbor Rosie's grandchildren, Joel and Ryan. They hovered over the strawberry patch as we picked, ready and willing to share the fruit. In fact, my mom still calls them "stowberries" – the mispronounced name created by two little boys. Those boys and I loved the Concord grapes that ripened each summer and we enjoyed the red raspberries growing in their grandmother's garden too.

Summer harvests, of both fruit and fun, are unforgettable. Take time to teach your children and grandchildren about the delights of the garden. Dig for potatoes, collect berries in a metal colander, pick apples by flashlight…whatever you do, do it together.

QUICK TIPS

✄ TIPS ON GROWING SMALL FRUITS ✄

Great balls of fruit

If you're looking for something that grows like a weed, try raspberries. Put them in average garden soil with full sun and look out. If planted early in the spring they may even produce fruit in their first season. After that, if pruned properly, raspberries will give you two crops a season: one in the late spring and one in the fall. In late winter remove any canes that have already fruited (you'll see the spent fruit clusters at the top of the stem) all the way down to the ground; these stems will not fruit again. Wait until new growth emerges along the remaining stems in early spring, then cut those canes down to just above the new growth; these stems will provide your early crop. The newest canes will emerge from the ground and go on to produce your autumn crop.

Great grapes

Grapes are another easy fruit to grow, as long as they are given full sun, support and are pruned correctly. The vines need something to grow on, like an arbor, trellis or fence: whatever you use, make sure that it's built to last. The vines will often outlive the gardener and it's tough to redo an arbor with a mass of vines covering it. Prune grapes hard in late winter by following each stem back to where it meets the main "trunk." Then backtrack up the stem, counting nodes (or buds) as you go. Cut the stem back just above the third node. Prevent fungal diseases early and often with one of the organic fungicides we recommend in Chapter 9.

Blueberries to die for

Blueberries are great fun to grow. They are relatively pest and disease free and they provide many years of reliable production. Plant several varieties with different maturation dates so you'll be harvesting from mid-summer through fall. There is no special trick to pruning blueberries; in fact, lots of folks don't do it at all. Just be aware that blueberries form their fruit on the previous year's growth, so if you cut off too much, you may be removing potential fruit. Only cut out dead wood and, at most, half of the old, woody stems.

Blueberries on acid

Blueberries are one of few non-evergreen plants preferring acidic soil. A pH of 4.5-4 is ideal. Test your soil as recommended in Chapter 3 and lower the pH with additions of elemental sulfur.

Simple strawberries

Plant bare root strawberries in early spring and remove any flowers they produce for the first year. This allows them to establish a good root system and to increase production in following years. The most common problem with strawberries is botrytis, a fungal disease that turns the ripening fruit into a ball of fuzzy mush. There isn't much you can do about it except make sure your strawberries have plenty of room to grow, mulch with straw between the plants to keep the berries off the ground, and hope for drier conditions. Some of the organic fungicides we detail in Chapter 9 will help control it too.

Making more strawberries

Strawberries reproduce by sending out runners. The runners form new plants that can, and should, be removed from the parent and planted elsewhere. Since most strawberry plants remain productive for only a few years, plant the babies in a different area to ensure you'll have a new crop when the mother plants stop fruiting. When they are spent, pull out the mother plants, work some compost in the soil and replant the following year with yet more babies.

Winter mulch

Most strawberries prefer a light winter covering of straw or shredded leaves placed right on top of them. It affords a bit of extra protection through the colder months, but the mulch will need to be removed in early spring to help prevent rot.

❧ MORE GOOD PRACTICES ❧

Thinning fruit

Thin your fruit trees by removing some of the crop about a month after the fruit has set. Thinning is performed for several reasons: to increase the size of the remaining fruit, to keep the branches from cracking under the weight of excessive fruit, to maximize the air circulation (thereby reducing disease) and to keep fruit trees bearing every year (most un-thinned fruit trees will produce decent crops only every other year). Thin apples, peaches, nectarines, apricots, plums and pears by leaving only one fruit every 6 inches and choosing the largest, healthiest specimens for maturity.

A little help from our friends

A cover crop of hairy vetch, crimson or white clover planted between rows in the orchard will attract beneficial insects and pollinators, fix nitrogen in the soil and keep weeds down. Plus, it doesn't need to be mowed nearly as often as grass.

Smart choice

When selecting varieties of peaches, apricots and nectarines pay attention to their bloom time. Early flowering varieties are more prone to damage from a late frost. If you live in a northern clime, late blooming cultivars are your best bet.

Mulch ring

Give your trees a bit of a buffer. Surround the trunks with a wide ring of mulch (making sure it doesn't touch the trunk itself). This "moat" will serve as protection from the lawn mower and string trimmer. And it will allow you to easily examine the bark for signs of borers and other damage.

❧ USEFUL GADGETS ❧

Bag o' fruit

To make apple picking easier, buy an orchard harvest bag. These bags are made of heavy-duty fabric with a long padded strap – supporting the weight around your full body and not just on a single arm. Wear one and you can pick with both hands, dropping the fruit gently into the bag as you go. Easily released with two simple clips, the folded bottom empties the contents in a flash.

A quality sprayer

One of the first purchases for the home orchard is a good sprayer. Depending on the size of your orchard (and trees) you can buy a sprayer that only holds a few quarts for $50 or a backpack sprayer that will run you $150. Whichever type you choose, make sure it has replaceable parts and comes with some sort of warranty. Don't "under buy" a sprayer; you will be using it often and will appreciate higher quality.

For the birds

Protect blueberries, strawberries and other small fruits from birds by covering the plants with bird netting. You can build a frame from PVC pipe or untreated lumber, cover it with netting and place it over the plants. Make the frame portable so you can use it only until the harvest is complete.

Roll the tape

There's a product called scare tape that can be strung through cherry trees as they ripen. Its reflective surface helps repel birds, but some old-timers swear that aluminum pie pans hung from the tree are still the best method.

Stretch

Even with the best pruning techniques, trees can get too tall to easily pick. Try a fruit harvester. It's basically a long pole topped by a small metal basket with protruding "fingers" to claw-off and catch the fruit. You can also make your own by using a large coffee can lined with soft foam or quilt batting.

Don't jump

There's a special ladder designed with a wider base for use in orchards. Using this ladder is a safer way to get up to the best-looking fruit (it's always at the top, isn't it?) without injuring the tree or yourself.

Tree goop

For years we were taught to apply a sealant to tree wounds and pruning cuts. Experts tell us now that it's best just to let the injury heal itself, without the help of a dressing.

✄ MORE ORCHARD CRITTERS ✄

Rabbits

Rabbits love to chew bark, especially when other food sources are scarce. They can be stopped by a short fence made from hardware cloth or chicken wire surrounding the trunk of the tree.

Those darned deer

If antler-rubbing bucks are a problem in your orchard and the area can't be fenced off, surround the trunk with something coarse, like metal gutter guards or a plastic corrugated drainage pipe. You can also wrap a 2-foot-long section of the trunk with aluminum foil – even though it would come off with the first rub, the deer don't seem to want to touch it.

Nibblin' deer

Deer will feast on the tender shoots of fruit trees, especially during the winter and early spring. Protect young trees by placing a sturdy box-wire fence around each one. For mature trees, spray regularly with a deer deterrent or remove lower branches (though this will make for a more difficult harvest, as all the fruit will now be higher up).

ADVANCED QUICK TIPS

❧ FUNKY FRUIT ❧

A taste of New Zealand

For something a little different, try growing hardy kiwis. They come in fuzzed and fuzzless varieties and some ornamental varieties even have variegated foliage. Plants are either male or female, so to produce fruit you'll need to be sure you have at least one male plant for every 3 or 4 females. Be sure the varieties are compatible for pollination. Kiwis are vigorous climbers and need to have a sturdy arbor or trellis to twine around.

What in the heck is a pawpaw?

This tree was a favorite of Native Americans because it produces a fruit with a creamy texture reminiscent of a banana or mango (hence one of its nicknames: The Indiana Banana). Pawpaws are an under-story tree and prefer to grow along a wood's edge or under the canopy of larger trees. Though they are relatively easy to grow, they do need another pawpaw to serve as a cross-pollinator; and they can take several years to bear fruit. The flowers are slightly fragrant (by that we mean slightly stinky) and don't always attract many of the flies and beetles that typically pollinate them. Some growers resort to placing trays of rotting meat near the plants to attract more flies.

Quince

Once a common fruit, quince has fallen out of vogue. We figure it must be because of the tart tasting fruit, since the trees in flower are absolutely amazing and they are relatively easy to grow. Fruiting quince is a different species from its shrubby flowering cousin, though the lower types do occasionally set small fruits. Quince fruits are most commonly made into jam and jelly, but it occasionally crops up as an ingredient in other recipes.

Heirloom fruit

It can be fun to grow the same varieties of fruit our ancestors enjoyed. Want to grow a variety from yesteryear?   Plant an heirloom.   Many of them are naturally disease resistant, tasty and productive. Heritage, or heirloom, varieties come in different shapes and flavors, ranging from very sweet to extremely tart.   The Arkansas Black apple dates back to 1886 and has dark purple (almost black) fruit with crisp, coarse flesh and a sharp flavor.   Donut peaches have been in cultivation for over 400 years; they are a unique flat-shaped peach with a sunken center and a fabulous, sweet taste.   Check out the Friends of the Organic Gardener appendix for sources.

Morels and orchards

It's a well-known fact that morel mushrooms have a symbiotic relationship with apple trees. Each spring mushroom hunters look for old orchards and pick the tasty morels from their "secret" location.   But, unless you're an expert, we suggest you refrain from collecting any mushrooms in your garden or orchard – some are very dangerous and may even be deadly.

✖ FURTHER PROTECTION ✖

Jack Frost

When a late frost threatens to zap your apricot or peach blossoms, turn on the sprinkler. By keeping the flowers wet when the temperatures freeze, they will be under a protective layer of ice. It sounds strange, but this actually protects the blossoms from frost damage. The sprinkler will have to run all night and into the morning, when the rising sun will help warm the tree.

✄ GRAFTING ✄

The many faces of Eve

Ever see an ad for one of those apple trees with five different types of apples? How 'bout a tree that grows peaches, plums and apricots together? It's accomplished by a technique called grafting. Most of today's apples are grafted onto hardy rootstocks to increase their vigor, but these multi-variety trees are unique. A single bud from an apple tree of each of the different varieties is inserted under the bark of the "mother" tree. They are united in such a way that they continue to grow together. Varieties are chosen for their bloom times, to promote proper pollination and for compatibility; sorry, you can't graft a pear onto an apple. The second combo we mention above consists of all stone fruit, some of which are indeed compatible.

Pick your poison

Some fruit tree catalogs will actually let you choose the rootstock you'd like your trees grafted onto. Most of today's fruit is grown on a different root system, improving hardiness and passing on the dwarfing trait. If you need something else from your rootstock, peruse these catalogs and read the details and benefits of each different rootstock, then choose accordingly.

Graft your own

Grafting is really an art. If you'd like to try your hand at it, contact a local botanic garden or orchard to sign up for a class. They will teach you all about choosing compatible varieties and how the different kinds of graft unions work. Once you know how to do it, experiment and have fun.

✄ AND NOW FOR SOMETHING COMPLETELY DIFFERENT ✄

Seeds of change

If you're up for a decade-long adventure and have lots of room, try growing apples from seed. It can be a challenge and the resulting apples will not resemble their parent, but this is exactly how many great apples are "discovered."

8

THE ORGANIC LAWN
TURF MANAGEMENT MADE EASY

A lawn is nature under totalitarian rule.
— MICHAEL POLLAN

If you live in a neighborhood where lawns matter, you understand the importance of deep green, weed-free grass. In this chapter we'll discuss how to attain perfection for your home turf *without* using nasty chemicals. When all is said and done, you'll finally be able to enjoy one of life's greatest pleasures: walking barefoot through your own organic paradise.

The American Ideal

American lawns have become a status symbol; the perfect, picturesque suburban house is inevitably fronted with an impeccable lawn. As a nation, we are willing to spend millions every year to attain and maintain this ideal of perfection. No other country in the world spends as much for an impressive green spread as we do. As a result, our yards are doused with dangerous pesticides, saturated with synthetic fertilizers and over-irrigated. And our lawns have become one of the worst sources of runoff pollution; those chemical fertilizers, herbicides and pesticides wash down into our storm drains and eventually find their way into our streams, rivers and lakes. What makes little sense is that homeowners are using more chemicals per acre than big agriculture; and we aren't even producing food, we're producing an image.

As gardeners, we understand what a perfect lawn stands for; we understand why people want it. It's beautiful and it feels good to look out the window and watch the kids playing ball on our own little patch of green. But it's now time we realize the dangers of the methods we've been relying on to achieve this perfection. And it's even more important that we find ways to safely and correctly achieve that beautiful, weed-free lawn we so desire. A recent study published in the Journal of the National Cancer Institute finds that household and garden pesticide use can increase the risk of childhood leukemia nearly sevenfold.

What feels even better than finally attaining the perfect lawn? The knowledge that you are succeeding without jeopardizing the health and wellbeing of your children, your pets, your environment and yourself.

We won't kid you, growing an organic lawn isn't easy. But it *is* possible, and once you convert your lawn to natural care, we guarantee you plenty of satisfaction. Watching the family gaze at the clouds, seeing Rover roll in the grass, wrestling with your toddler in the front yard – all of this will bring deeper meaning to your new organic garden.

Great Grass! – establishing a new lawn

The surest way to get a great organic lawn is to start from scratch. That won't come as good news if you already have an established lawn, but your old lawn likely carries a lot of baggage – like low soil fertility or a high weed count – and it's best to start with a clean slate.

The most important component of your new organic lawn is going to be the condition of the soil beneath it. Trust us, it's worth the extra effort to get the dirt in shape. Everything you do with your lawn from now on will be determined by the choices you make in improving the soil.

Soil Test – We told you in Chapter 3 how to take a soil test; this should be your very first step. The results will give you a good baseline and will help you establish what nutrients need to be added to your soil and if any pH change needs to be made. For help in determining how best to prepare your soil, we suggest a full review of Chapter 3; and of course we recommend adding plenty of the main ingredient: organic matter. Whether it's well-aged manure, crumbly leaf mold, or sweet black compost, starting with rich soil will prevent a multitude of problems down the road.

Soil Prep – Begin your soil preparation by adding about 2 inches of organic matter to the soil surface. Next, till the entire area and then rake smooth, removing all the rocks and other refuse. There are special aluminum rakes with very wide, sturdy tines, made specifically for raking a new lawn area. These are lightweight, easy to use and well worth the investment.

Seeding – Spring is a great time to seed the lawn, as long as soil temperature is 50 degrees or above. Though we prefer spring or early fall, seeding can be done through most of the season if temperatures are not too extreme, *and* there's proper moisture for germination. The condition and variety of grass seed you plant can make a huge impact on the health of your organic lawn. Choose a good quality seed, one that is fresh, weed-free and right for the conditions of your new lawn. In other words, if your new lawn will be in a shady location, don't buy a variety of grass that is meant for full sun. Your local nursery or feed store should be able to assist you in making the proper seed selection. You can find some of our favorite sources for organically grown grass seed mixes listed in the appendix.

Keep an eye out for a very desirable grass seed that is labeled "endophyte enhanced." This seed contains a naturally occurring fungus that helps the plant produce compounds that ward off insect attacks. The presence of the fungus helps increase the vigor and hardiness of the grass. It makes the plants more resistant to pests like chinch bugs, armyworms, webworms and aphids and is considered a natural biological control (more about these in Chapter 9). It is worth your time to seek out endophyte enhanced seed. You should *not* plant it, however, if there will be any livestock grazing in the area; it is not good forage.

Seeding the lawn is pretty easy; you can do it by hand or with a spreader. We like to distribute about 1/4 of the total seed amount first, and then go over the area a couple more times in different directions, sowing the remainder. Lightly rake the seed into the soil – good contact between the seed and the soil is essential for high germination. Water the area thoroughly. Apply enough water to get the seed wet, but not enough to drown it or wash it away. This is a critical time for the seed. If it is allowed to dry out before or shortly after germination it will not survive.

To help protect the seed and the new emerging seedling, use a light coating of straw or hay to shield the seeds from marauding birds and to keep the soil moist. If you've got it, you can also use sifted compost or another organic matter for the same purpose. Hopefully, you'll get some help from Mother Nature in the form of rain; if not, keep the area moist until a few weeks after germination.

Keep off the lawn for the first month of its life. After that, it's fine to cut it, but be sure your mower has a sharp blade.

Extreme Lawn Makeover – improving an existing lawn

If you are beginning your organic lawn conversion with an established plot, admittedly you have a bit more work on your hands. And you'll need more patience, but we assure you, it's all worth it.

The biggest concern in converting an existing conventional lawn is what to do about the weeds. If the lawn is newly installed, there may not be many weeds. In that case, weed prevention is of the utmost importance; it is much easier to keep them from moving in than it is to eradicate them once they've taken hold. For this purpose you'll need to use an organic pre-emergent herbicide called *corn gluten meal*. A by-product of the corn milling process, corn gluten meal is a granular substance that is applied with a spreader. Though it will not rid your grass of existing weeds, it will prevent any new weed seedlings from germinating by drying out the plant's initial root. When used properly, it's the perfect foil for crabgrass, dandelions and many other weeds. And it's a great source of nitrogen fertilizer as well. Be careful though, as it prevents *all* seeds from sprouting, not just weed seeds. Don't re-seed a lawn and then treat it with corn gluten; your grass seed will not come up. Wait 5 to 6 weeks after applying the meal to re-seed your lawn; or hold off on applying it until after your newly planted grass is a few inches high. Corn gluten should be spread in the spring around the time the Forsythia bloom, and then again in the fall. After two years of treatment the product is over 90% effective – comparable to the success rate of many chemical weed-n-feeds.

Established weeds in your turf grass can be very discouraging; they are the biggest stumbling block for those converting their lawn to organic care. Folks just don't want to deal with them. Eradicating pernicious, perennial weeds like dandelions, thistle, clover and others can seem a daunting task – particularly in the lawn. Although hand pulling is the most effective technique, it can also be time consuming. As a result, we recommend spot treating the worst areas. This may seem extreme to those of you who are plagued with trailing weeds, like ground ivy or spurge, but it will allow you to get rid of the weeds and start from scratch in any areas that are heavily infested.

Spot treating can be done in a couple of ways. For a large area of weedy lawn, you can use an organic herbicide. Be aware that this will kill the grass in addition to the weeds, so you will need to re-seed after the treatment. If the weeds are scattered here and there throughout the lawn, apply the herbicide only in the small area where the weeds are located, then re-seed. For scattered weeds, here is another method: wear rubber gloves, covered by a pair of cotton ones; then spray the outer, fabric gloves with the organic herbicide and run your gloved hands over the weeds. This will deliver the herbicide where you want it, and it may prevent some runoff onto the grass. For very mature perennial weeds, two applications may be necessary. We have some favorite clove oil-based organic herbicides, and we've listed sources in the appendix.

Happy and Healthy

The best technique for a weed-free lawn is to grow a healthy lawn. Strong, vigorous, organically grown grass will out-compete any weeds. It will be more resistant to any pests, have a root system up to 3 feet deep (!) and need less fertilization and water. At the end of this chapter, we outline a seasonal lawn care regimen that will help you build and maintain the strong, thick turf we all covet.

Maintenance Matters

To keep the lawn growing optimally, you may want to add a bit of organic fertilizer in the spring and again in the fall. We love compost for this purpose because it will not only provide a good balance of nutrients, but it will do so over a long period of time. The compost will also add organic matter to the soil and help feed the microbes that break down thatch (more about thatch later). Finely screened compost can be applied with a drop spreader or even with a shovel or pitchfork. The idea is to put down about 1/4 inch of compost twice a year, scattered into the grass. It will be more than enough to keep the lawn growing at the perfect rate and will help provide nice color and balanced root and leaf growth.

You may prefer to use a granular organic fertilizer on your grass – a bit less cumbersome to spread than compost, and the nutritional analysis is pretty much guaranteed. There are wonderful organic 4-step programs that are high-lighted in the appendix, and we highly recommend them. These products work to prevent weeds, feed your grass and build the health of your soil, just like conventional weed-n-feeds (only there are no derivatives of Agent Orange in the organic version).

Mowing – The health of your lawn is determined in part by the *way* the grass is cut. Cut the grass to a height of about 3 to 3 1/2 inches. By keeping the grass tall, you're shading out many of the weeds, and allowing plenty of sur-face area for photosynthesis. Plus, the stronger and longer the plant's top growth is, the stronger and longer the plant's roots are – meaning it will be more able to access its own nutrients and water from the soil, and will be less dependent on you. Never let it grow too long before cutting; if you remove more than 1/3 the total blade length you will scalp the grass, which may make it more susceptible to disease. Very important: be sure to sharpen mower blades at least once a year.

Grass clippings should be left to decompose into the soil. They break down quickly and add nutrients to the lawn, providing up to half of your lawn's total nitrogen needs. A mulching mower is perfect for this purpose; it uses a special blade and an enclosed deck to chop and evenly distribute the clip-pings. We are particularly fond of the saying, *Cut it high and let it lie.* Allow-ing those clippings to break down naturally not only provides nitrogen, but it prevents all those bags of grass from going to the landfill. Best of all, lawns mowed with mulching mowers have been found to have larger populations of the beneficial microbes that help break down thatch.

Watering – Even though we don't really consider watering the lawn a necessary part of an organic maintenance program, we feel the need to include
it here. Obviously, plenty of folks think it's an essential chore, or else there
would be no such thing as a sprinkler. Here's why it's anything but compul-
sory: grass is supposed to go dormant when temperatures rise and water is
scarce. It is supposed to turn brown: it's a part of its natural growth cycle.
Many varieties of turf grass actually thrive on having this summer period to
rest and rejuvenate themselves for winter. We believe that letting your grass
pass through this dormant phase will make it more winter hardy and resistant
to pests and pathogens.

We know that the lion's share of homeowners feel the need for year-round
green. So, if you are going to do it, you had better do it right; otherwise
you may be doing more harm than good. Do not let the sprinkler run for 10
minutes here and there – run it for as long as it takes to distribute an inch of
water (put a tuna can under the sprinkler's path; when it's full you've watered
an inch). If there is no natural rain, use the hose only once a week and apply
the whole inch in one dousing. This will ensure a deep, penetrating watering
that will encourage your plant's roots to grow deep enough to access plenty
of nutrients. Those deep roots will help reduce the need for fertilization and
further watering; a thriving root system can help keep the plants alive and
well even in drought conditions. And always water in the morning, which will
help suppress disease and fungus.

De-thatching and aerating – These two very helpful cultural practices
improve growth and the overall health of the grass. They should only be
done if necessary, however, and only every 3 to 4 years. We recommend
performing these tasks in the cool fall weather; this will allow the grass time
to rebound before active spring growth.

Thatch is a layer of roots and old stems that accumulates between the
growing plant and the soil surface. Thatch generally builds when excess
fertilizer and improper watering cause the plant to grow too quickly. It also
builds when there aren't enough microbes present to help break it down.
Too much thatch can prevent water, air and nutrients from getting to your
plants' roots. When you begin to convert your lawn to organic care, a good
de-thatching may be necessary. You'll know this by examining the soil's surface on your hands and knees. If the thatch is thicker than 1/2 inch, it's time

to de-thatch. Properly managed organic lawns seldom have excessive thatch, as they are fed at appropriate rates and host billions of beneficial microbes.

A special machine can be used for de-thatching; we recommend renting one with a neighbor. You share the cost and ensure your neighbor's lawn won't bring the property values down. The job can also be done with a special hand rake, but we would only recommend that for small lawns and strong backs.

Aerating uses another type of machine. It perforates the lawn, removing cores of soil and leaving small plugs strewn across the grass. This is great for high traffic areas where the soil has been compacted. The resulting holes allow nutrients and water to get to the roots of the grass and they help break up heavily trodden soil. To get rid of the plugs, let them dry out for a day and then use the mower to make quick work of them. They will become a source of nutrients for the lawn as they break down.

Fall leaf cleanup – another important maintenance task for your organic lawn. There are a few ways to deal with fall leaves: rake them off, collect them with a lawn sweeper or shred them with a mulching mower. It's imperative to remove all the fallen leaves, otherwise they tend to mat on the lawn, suffocating it and promoting disease. Along with that fall cleanup should come a final mowing. Your last cut of the season should be about 1/2 inch shorter than usual. This will prevent the grass from collapsing under snow cover and becoming a harbor for pathogens.

A Few Pitfalls

One big mistake homeowners make is to repeatedly use a high nitrogen fertilizer. Yes, it gives you instant green, but it also makes the grass blades more susceptible to disease and insect damage. Use a balanced organic fertilizer on the lawn; it makes the plant stronger overall by not only promoting top growth, but root growth as well.

Probably the number one question we hear on our radio show is, "How do I deal with grubs in my lawn?" Grubs are the larval stage of Japanese beetles and these critters love to feed on the roots of common turf grass. To find out if they are a problem in your lawn, use a spade to turn over one square foot of sod. Examine the roots and if you find the area is infested with 10 or more grubs, you've got a problem. This is the only way to ensure that the grubs are the reason for your brown, patchy lawn and not something else.

Milky spore or *Bacillus popillae* is a wonderful organic control for grubs. It's a naturally occurring bacterium that infects and kills the grub (and only the grub – it doesn't harm any other soil life or mammals). Milky spore is granular and is spread on the lawn's surface. As the dead grub decomposes, it releases billions of new spores. The great thing about milky spore is that it stays in the soil for years and spreads over time – one application remains effective for up to 15 years.

Along with grubs, usually come moles. These little guys are a natural control for grubs, and are usually considered a good thing. They do not feed on plants, so if they are tunneling through your flowerbeds or lawn, let them be. They are eating grub after grub, aerating the soil and leaving a little fertilizer to boot.

There may be times when your lawn is plagued by fungal diseases: snow mold, brown patch, dollar spot and blights – to name a few. These diseases are brought on by wet, humid weather, improper fertilization, excess watering and other inappropriate maintenance techniques. Following the lawn care regimen we highlight at the end of this chapter will help prevent many of these diseases from taking hold. Properly caring for your turf and allowing the plants to build their own immunities are the best methods of handling fungal diseases. There are organic fungicides available for use on turf grass, but there is a difference of opinion about their effectiveness. Fortunately, fungal diseases don't usually kill a lawn; your lawn may just look bad for a while until conditions improve. See the Quick Tips section for a few more ideas on dealing with specific fungal issues organically.

A perfect organic lawn is not effortless. But rest assured, even though it might take two or more seasons for the grass to reach perfection, you'll clearly earn your bragging rights – both for the gorgeous green you've created and the earth you've helped to protect. Impressing those neighbors has never been so satisfying.

ANNUAL ORGANIC LAWN-CARE REGIMEN

Early Spring

1. Sharpen and balance mower blades. Change your mower's spark plugs, oil and air filter.
2. Rake up any leaves, sticks and other refuse, or mow the leaves with a mulching mower.
3. Begin regular mowing as soon as grass resumes growth.
4. Apply corn gluten meal at manufacturer's recommended rate.
5. Take a soil test. Find out your soil's pH and fertility levels. Use the results to determine your fertilizer choices. Review Chapter 3 for more info on soil testing.

Spring

1. Re-seed bare spots 5 to 6 weeks after any corn gluten application. Water these areas religiously until grass is established.
2. Pull young weeds or spot treat, as needed. Dig up any dandelions while they are easy to find and before they go to seed.
3. Apply a balanced granular organic fertilizer or distribute 1/4 inch of compost onto the lawn.
4. Test for grub population. If 10 or more per square foot are encountered, spread milky spore over the entire lawn area.
5. Watch for fungal issues. If you notice a problem, dig out infected turf and soil immediately. Fill in the void with a mix of topsoil and compost, then re-seed.

Summer

1. Continue to remove any weeds that should emerge.
2. Water only if you feel it absolutely necessary, or allow the grass to pass into natural summer dormancy.
3. Mow regularly to a height of 3 to 3 1/2 inches.
4. Continue to watch for disease.
5. Test again for grub populations if you notice any damage.

Late Summer

1. Spread another application of corn gluten meal.

2. Do one final fertilization in mid-August using a balanced organic granular fertilizer (many organic gardeners feel this fertilization to be unnecessary – we think it depends on the results of your spring soil test).

3. Continue to spot treat for established weeds and do not allow them to set seed.

Fall

1. Aerate if needed.

2. Top dress with 1/4 inch of compost if you did not apply any granular fertilizer in mid-August.

3. Remove all leaves by raking or mowing them.

4. De-thatch the lawn by mid-September, but only if needed. This will allow the grass time to rebound while soil temperatures remain warm.

5. Perform one final mowing to a height of 2 1/2 inches.

6. Apply lime to lawns with a high soil pH. Please read the pH section of Chapter 3 for more information.

7. Drain the mower of gas and store appropriately.

Winter

1. Take your mower into the shop for a maintenance check.

2. Continue to examine your lawn for molds and fungus. Remove any matted leaves or snow.

Doug Tells All | *about his "quilted lawn"*

I'm often asked what to do about violets growing in the lawn. My shocking response: enjoy them. Pick the flowers and use them in salads.

You see, I don't care about the perfect lawn. I live in the woods and as long as it's green, that's OK with me. For me, nothing grows better than grass. I refer to my yard as a "quilted lawn" because it is filled with a diverse variety of plants – clover, violets, crabgrass and the like.

Don't get me started on dandelions – they are one of the most nutritious food sources on the planet. A pest? Not in my book. The early spring greens are a bitter treasure for salads, sautéed with garlic or used with tomato sauce on pizza. Yet the plant is considered a scourge of the lawn; the most reviled weed of all. How ironic that something filled with so many vitamins and minerals (and, yes, even beauty) causes homeowners to unload a deluge of herbicides (most of which probably end up in our drinking water).

If the lawn gets to the point that I can't stand it, I will apply corn gluten in the fall and spring to help the lawn bounce back. It has to get really bad though for me to make the effort. I cut my grass every couple of weeks; I leave it high and use a simple trick that works well in every corner of the garden: I ignore the weeds. I just look right through them to the containers filled with impatiens and floppy red begonias or over to the arbor of white clematis.

Appreciating the beauty of the garden and the lawn is all a matter of which direction you're looking.

Jess Tells All — *about going Dutch*

Do you remember when you were a kid and sweet smelling white Dutch clover covered all the neighborhood lawns? I loved watching the honeybees searching each little globular flower for nectar. Years ago, white Dutch clover was included in all the grass mixes sold at feed stores and garden centers. Unfortunately, this one-time standard is now considered a weed. Chemical companies couldn't develop a product that would eradicate the dandelions without harming the clover (a broad leaf weed killer will eliminate anything that doesn't have flat blades like grass). And so it was decided that clover is no longer desirable. I can't help but feel that we'd all be better off behaving like the children we once were and appreciating every little sweet, white blossom.

Having an ample population of white clover in amongst your grass is one of the easiest ways to ensure a healthy, vigorous lawn. Here's why: clover actually converts nitrogen from the air into a form that the grass can use. Basically, it provides a natural, readily available form of fertilizer (especially true if you use a mulching mower). The clover also keeps plenty of those pollinating bees and other beneficial insects in the yard. And its presence prevents the lawn from being a monoculture – that way, if disease strikes it will be less likely to spread. You'll cut down on water consumption too; lawns with clover generally have deeper roots and show more overall vigor. White Dutch can also help choke out weeds, covering bare areas quickly and overtaking invading plants like spotted spurge and plantain. Helping to break up heavy clay soils, clover is also great forage for rabbits, groundhogs and deer. You may scoff at this last point, but I have seen many of these animals feeding on the clover in my lawn instead of the vegetables and flowers in my garden. They much prefer clover to ornamentals.

White clover can bring tons of luck to the organic gardener. Not only in the form of a few four-leaf clovers, but also in the form of more time to spend with the family – instead of with the lawn spreader.

QUICK TIPS

❧ MOWING ❧

The final cut

Your last mow of the season should be about 1/2 inch shorter than usual. This helps prevent the grass blades from falling over and getting matted down under snow cover.

Earth's choice

If you just have a small city lot, use a reel mower instead of a gas guzzler. These hand-powered tools have come a long way over the last few decades. Newer models are incredibly easy to use, rolling smoothly and bearing sharp, low maintenance blades.

String trimmers

Sloped areas of the lawn may be difficult to access with a mower. For these places, we recommend buying an electric string trimmer or hand trimming by using a short handled brush whacker.

Don't cut when wet

Cutting the grass when it's wet is the same as mowing with a dull blade. Wet grass will tear, providing an entry point for pathogens and disease.

Its cool, baby

Mow in the cool morning or evening – this will cause your grass (and you) the least amount of stress.

Robots on the lawn?

Do you hate cutting the grass as much as we do? There are several companies that make a relatively inexpensive robot (around $800) that will cut the grass for you. Just set up the perimeter with a special wire and let the robot loose on the lawn. The robot works best on flat lawns and is powered by a rechargeable battery. Wish they would invent one that would do the weeding too.

Following directions

When you mow your lawn, try not to travel in the same direction every time. This can cause the more slender types of grass to bend and lie in the direction of the mow. They will then be more reluctant to stand upright and may become matted.

Get rid of it

Do we really need so much lawn? Why not replace a section with a wildflower blend or native groundcover? No one we know actually likes to mow the lawn and eliminating just a few feet of it can cut down on mowing time and maintenance requirements.

✂ FERTILIZING ✂

Compost

Spreading compost on the lawn can seem like a daunting task. Here's an easy way to get it done. Fill a wheelbarrow with compost, breaking up any large clumps as you go. Using a short-handled, flat-bladed pitch fork (also called a border fork), fling the compost on to the lawn. Use a quick snapping motion to distribute the compost evenly.

Escape! Escape!

Even organic fertilizers that spill onto the driveway or end up in a pile on the grass should be swept up and collected. If left in a concentrated pile on the grass they may cause foliage burns; nor do we want it washing into the storm sewer.

✄ MAINTENANCE ✄

Grass clippings

If you like to collect your grass clippings to use as mulch in the veggie garden, invest in a lawn sweeper. These gizmos attach to the back of the lawn tractor and collect the clippings as you mow. You can dump them right next to the garden gate.

Seeding made easy

When re-seeding the bare spots in your lawn, don't be tempted to over-apply. Grass seedlings need plenty of space. A good rule of thumb is to sprinkle the seed until there is a fingernail's width between each one. Any closer than that and they'll crowd each other for air and water.

✄ WEEDY ISSUES ✄

Beat the weeds

To force out the weeds, try a technique called over-seeding. Here's how: spread a bit of seed on an undisturbed lawn. Run a verticutter machine (used for de-thatching) through the lawn and then spread more seed. This will invigorate the lawn with new young growth.

Timing is everything

Be vigilant and pull weeds before they go to seed. But remember, no yard is going to be completely weed-free. Embrace that idea and live with it; you'll feel better if you do.

Plantain

Weedy plantain species that grow in the lawn are much easier to pull by hand when they are in bloom. For some reason the roots give up their grip more readily when there are flower stalks on top. Go figure.

✄ TROUBLE ✄

Another grub control

Use beneficial nematodes in the spring to control the larval stage of Japanese beetles. These nematodes are naturally occurring microscopic worms that kill root-eating grubs and are not harmful to humans, pets or plants. They are sold in sponges that are soaked in water and sprinkled on the lawn. See the appendix for sources.

Check out the 'shrooms

People often ask us how to get rid of mushrooms in the lawn. They really don't cause any harm and are some of nature's best decomposers. If they bother you, just rake them away. Never eat a mushroom in the wild, but do get on your hands and knees and examine them. They are one of nature's most fascinating creations.

Fido's revenge

Your lawn is now a lush, deep green oasis only rivaled by the greens at Pebble Beach. Then you see Fido relieving himself on your precious turf. The resulting burn spots on the lawn may make you want to go Ralph Kramden. But relax, it's only grass. After years of study, our professional opinion is to do nothing. That's right, just let the tall grass around the offending spot grow in and cover it. Over time, rain will rinse the excess nitrogen away and the grass will creep back. If you really can't stand it, soak the area with water soon after your pup relieves himself. This will help dilute the urine, eliminating the potential for burn.

Sunflowers and grass

If you put a bird feeder in your lawn and fill it with sunflowers, the grass beneath it will eventually die. The seed coats of sunflowers contain a compound that prevents other plants from growing (it's called allelopathy) so to prevent a bare spot in the lawn be sure to move the feeder every week or two.

⊱ CREEP AND CRAWL ⊰

Earthworms

Nothing says "organic lawn" more than a healthy earthworm population. You'll know you've got one when the driveway is crawling after a heavy rain.

Encouraging our squirmy friends

Help your local earthworms by adding organic matter to your lawn on an annual basis if possible. Pelletized or fresh compost is best, but leaf mold and mushroom soil work too.

ADVANCED QUICK TIPS

⊱ THE BIRDS AND THE BEES ⊰

Let the birds do the work

We've already mentioned how valuable birds can be for controlling pests in the veggie and flower garden, but they also love to eat some of those feeding on your lawn. To attract birds, plant easy-to-grow trees and shrubs like Viburnums, crabapples and beautyberries. And remember, birds will always appreciate having a water source and feeder nearby.

Ground bees

Ground nesting yellow jackets and wasps can be very aggressive, especially in the autumn. These insects are not the same as honeybees, as they build their nests in ground cavities. If you see the insects flying in and out of a hole in the grass, be sure to stay several feet away from the area. Contact an exterminator who can use natural powdered pyrethrins to get rid of the nest.

❧ FIGHTING TEA ❧

Drink your tea

Watering your lawn with compost tea will help prevent disease, because the solution contains millions of disease fighting, immune boosting beneficial microbes. Make the tea by steeping a few shovels of compost wrapped in burlap in 10 gallons of water. Apply it to areas prone to fungal attacks or use a pump sprayer to put it on the entire lawn.

❧ AERATING ❧

Crampons

Some catalogs sell footwear with spikes that attach to the bottom of your shoes. They are meant to aerate your lawn as you walk on it by piercing the soil surface. Unfortunately, they also push the surrounding soil together, compacting it even further. In our opinion, the only way to properly aerate your soil is to rent the machine that fully draws the cigar-shaped plugs out of the turf.

For easier aerating

Thoroughly water your lawn about two days before aerating. This will enable the machine's tines to penetrate the soil effortlessly and it will make the soil cores fall out easier.

❧ AT LEAST IT'S GREEN... ❧

Weeds and fertility

There are a few books on the market that teach you how to determine fertility problems in your soil based on the species of weeds that are growing in your lawn. It's a very interesting science and it makes a lot of sense. It might help you to learn a bit about your soil without needing to rely on a soil test every year. One book we like is *Weeds: Control Without Poisons*, by Charles Walters.

Moss

The presence of moss in your lawn may indicate a fertility or pH problem. Get your soil tested (the appendix provides sources). If it's in a shady area, be sure to re-seed with a mix heavy in fescue; it thrives in shadier conditions. We don't necessarily think moss is a bad thing – at least it's green!

❧ OF MOLDS AND MILDEWS ❧

Those handy bacteria

Bacillius pumilus is a naturally occurring bacterium that is used to battle many fungal diseases, including those of the lawn. Chapter 9 will tell you more about this biological fungicide and how it is best used.

Stop that mold

Many species of lawn mildews can be controlled with potassium bicarbonate products. These work by causing an imbalance in the pathogen's cells and result in collapsed cell walls. Several commercial brands are labeled for use on lawns. See the appendix for sources.

Citrus and mint

Botanical fungicides made from the oils of mint and citrus can be quite effective against many lawn diseases.

Snow mold

Snow mold can develop in years with heavy, prolonged snow cover. It's best prevented by collecting fall leaves and making your final cut a bit shorter than usual. To remedy snow mold, simply dig out smaller patches and re-seed or treat larger patches with an organic fungicide.

9

CONTROL ISSUES
NATURAL PEST MANAGEMENT STRATEGIES

By the time one is eighty, it is said, there is no longer a tug of
war in the garden…all is at last in balance and all is serene.
The gardener is usually dead, of course.
— HENRY MITCHELL, *THE ESSENTIAL EARTHMAN*

You've hauled 40 wheelbarrows of compost, planted every species of flowering herb known to man, fertilized properly, and…well, the pests came anyway. In this chapter we'll tell you precisely what you need to do to send those little buggers packing.

Pest Panic!

We've taken care of enough organic gardens over the years to know that just because you've improved the soil, used sound cultural practices and lured beneficial insects into the garden, it doesn't mean there won't be problems to deal with. In an organic garden, careful consideration comes before any action. An important part of managing your garden naturally is understanding that some pests in the garden are inevitable and normal. If you recall in Chapter 4, when we discussed beneficial insects we introduced the cycle of predator and prey. There need to be some pest insects in the garden in order for these "good guys" to have a reason to stick around. That's why it's important to understand that the complete elimination of any pest from the garden is never the goal. Your aim should be to bring their numbers down to a tolerable level. What's sometimes difficult to understand is that as you proceed toward a more organic approach, and a complete removal of synthetic pesticides, your tolerance level will have to increase. You'll have to teach yourself not to panic.

For many people the "don't panic" part of organic pest management is the most challenging step; we've been taught for many years that one "bad bug" is one too many. Changing the way we think about pests begins with understanding that every insect, no matter how seemingly vile, does indeed serve a purpose. It may simply be as lunch for another bug a tad higher on the food chain, or it may be as a pollinator (or the larva of one), or a decomposer. Whatever its reason for being, we need to respect it. That being said, we also are gardeners; we have invested time, patience, money and love into our garden and we do not want to see it be destroyed. Solving pest problems organically means finding that delicate balance between wanting our gardens to thrive and maintaining a bit of reverence for nature's process.

What "Damage" Really Means

Before reacting to any pest you encounter in the garden, examine exactly what it's doing and what kind of injury it's creating. There is a big difference between damage that simply mars the plant (aesthetic) and damage that cuts into your bottom line (economic). Often in an organic garden, feeding pests cause only minimal damage. The plant is not really suffering, it just doesn't look so hot. In aesthetic cases like this, it's best to simply prune out the affected parts or let the plant recover on its own; there's no need to take further action. Only when you feel the plant is in jeopardy, or there are financial repercussions, is there a real need to respond quickly. Economic cases might include issues in the veggie garden (you certainly save on food bills by growing your own) or damage to large, established landscape specimens (which enhance the value of your home). Allow the garden to fight some battles on its own. Unless there is a clear and obvious threat, stand back, but keep a close eye on the situation.

Pay attention to your garden. By watching it every day you can note how much has changed – if there is any new damage or if pest populations have increased. When you notice a problem, don't immediately raise the alarm. Observe the situation daily to see if the damage becomes intolerable. A keen, attentive eye is a superb form of garden defense.

The 6-Step Approach to Organic Pest Management

To help you obtain stability in the garden we have developed a simple 6-step approach to managing garden pests. It begins with ways to avoid the pest in the first place and ends with wise, organic solutions to persistent and challenging issues. It's important that each time you encounter a pest problem you proceed through the steps in order. This will enable you to gain a true understanding of the predicament and reduce the chances of its happening again. And, of course, it will also ensure the greatest chance of success, even on the first try.

This method is so successful because it works with nature instead of against it. And it works perfectly with all the guiding principals of organic gardening we discussed in Chapter 1. Plus, it's easy. Once you've formally followed the steps a few times, it will become second nature. Each time you encounter a pest, your mind will automatically proceed through each step and the solutions will become easier and easier to find...often without the spray bottle.

Step 1: Design the pest out of the garden

This is accomplished by choosing resistant varieties, properly spacing plants and placing them in conditions where they thrive. For example, if you constantly have problems with bacterial wilt on your cucumbers, plant varieties with proven resistance. By positioning your plants appropriately in the garden (i.e., shade lovers in the shade, bog plants in low lying areas, and natives in drought-prone sections) they will have healthier immune systems and will be better equipped to handle any problems. Don't crowd plants; inadequate air circulation can lead to fungal issues and it's easier for a bug to hop from one plant to the next. If you are battling a particular pest, think about whether the host plant is really thriving in its current location. You may decide to move it or replace it with a hardier variety. But when you feel the plant is sited correctly and is otherwise thriving (except for that darned bug!) then move to Step 2.

Step 2: Examine your actions (and the actions of other humans)

Take a good hard look at what you are doing in the garden. Perhaps you may be the cause of the problem: Are you maintaining good cultural practices in the garden? Are you fertilizing properly and taking good care of your soil? Are you pruning correctly? Sometimes it's just a matter of tweaking our own routine. Maybe you have slug problems because you've been watering at night instead of the morning; or perhaps you applied a fertilizer too high in nitrogen – this would cause a lot of tender green growth, which can be extra-tempting to pests. Have your gardening habits changed? Did you always clean up the garden at the end of the season, but now leave the debris to winter-over? Often, altering our own maintenance activities can alleviate a problem. If you can't find any inappropriate action on your part, then proceed to the next step.

Step 3: Verify, through thoughtful research, what the true problem is

Know thy enemy. Identify the insect, disease, weed or fungus causing the issue and learn about its lifecycle and habits. Use your resources – this is half the battle! There is no place in organic gardening for unstudied action; in other words, no spraying "just because it might help." You may have to trek into the garden at night, examine the undersides of the foliage, take your bug in a baggie to a local nursery or get a magnifying glass; by whatever means necessary you need to properly identify the culprit. Then learn about it and find out when it's most vulnerable. Some insects are better controlled during their larval stage (corn ear worm, Gypsy moth, squash vine borers and cabbage loopers) while others are susceptible as both larvae and adults (black vine weevil, flea beetles and Japanese beetles). There is no one "be-all, end-all" solution; each pest responds differently to its environment and consideration should be made to determine what and when a treatment will be most effective. Once you know who the perpetrator is you can begin to look for potential solutions by proceeding to Step 4.

Step 4: Determine if mechanical or physical controls will be effective

Many times a pest can be dealt with by using a little physical intervention. This can mean handpicking insects, using a sharp stream of water to knock them off the plants or trapping larger critters in a live trap. In the vegetable patch, floating row covers can be an extremely effective barrier. This lightweight spun fabric rests on top of the plants and prevents insects from landing to feed. How about pheromone traps in the orchard? These lures attract adult codling moths, then trap them on their sticky surface. The Quick Tip section of this chapter offers lots more helpful ideas for establishing physical control – including ideas for battling cutworms, cucumber beetles and even deer. If you can't find any physical or mechanical technique to rid yourself of your adversary, move on to Step 5.

Step 5: Are there biological controls that would work?

Biological controls involve using other living organisms to combat pests. In Chapter 4 you learned how to promote and attract appropriate beneficial insects to the garden on a consistent basis. Their effectiveness can be astounding. Other biological control methods include the use of naturally occurring bacteria to combat specific pests. What's great about these bacteria is that, when used properly, they only affect the targeted pest and they are very safe to use around beneficials. There are strains of these bacteria that suppress fungal issues like rusts, powdery mildew and fire blight; and many of them can be used on fruits and vegetables right up to the day of harvest. Some types are also effective against certain species of turf grass fungus. There are biological solutions for a remarkable number of pests (see the following section, Our Favorite Natural Pest Controls, for some choices), but if you are unable to find one to remedy your problem, proceed to Step 6 below.

Step 6: Apply an appropriate organic care product

Nine times out of ten you won't have to utilize this step – especially after the two-year transition period passes. It's often possible to remedy a problem before getting to this point – but if nothing else has been effective, start searching for an appropriate organic product. Make sure what you choose is suitable for the issue and always, always, *always* follow label instructions. To make this step easier and to ensure that you'll be making smart choices, we've included a list of our favorite organic controls and how best to use them. Remember, even though these products are generally safer to use than conventional sprays, they should be your last resort. Choose carefully and respect them. Just because they are natural, does not mean you should take exposure lightly. Protect yourself.

Our Favorite Natural Pest Controls

1. **Insecticides**

   A. *Botanical (derived from plant sources):*

   Neem – Made from the seeds of the tropical neem tree, this is really an all-purpose pesticide. It not only repels insects, but it suppresses feeding and prevents them from molting. Neem is effective against a broad range of insects including aphids, leafminers, loopers, sawfly larvae, four-lined plant bugs and mites, to name just a few. It is not harmful to humans, animals or soil life, but if applied incorrectly, it may be harmful to bees and other beneficials. Neem has fungicidal properties as well.

   Pyrethrins – A sometimes controversial organic pesticide, pyrethrins should be used only when absolutely necessary. They do harm beneficials and aquatic life so care must be taken with their application. Pyrethrin is derived from a species of chrysanthemum and acts against the pest's nervous system. It is an instant kill and is often used against wasp and yellow jacket nests. Be sure to select only natural pyrethrins and avoid their synthetic cousins, the pyrethroids – they are not organic. Pyrethrins are valued for combatting a huge number of pests including many types of beetles (potato, bean, blister, cucumber, asparagus and flea), loopers, caterpillars, thrips, earwigs, aphids and whiteflies.

   Garlic oil – Working as a pest repellent, garlic oil should be used as a preventive measure before pest populations begin to expand. It deters ants, aphids, cutworms, earworms, hornworms, leaf miners and others. Avoid spraying garlic oil when vegetables are in bloom – it will also repel those pollinating bees!

   Botanical essential oils – These are made from various plant oils including clove, wintergreen, cinnamon, rosemary and peppermint. Some forms of these pesticides control root pests like wireworms and cutworms, while others serve as foliar pesticides, eliminating aphids, potato beetles, loopers, mites, whiteflies and more. Very safe and surprisingly effective.

B. *Biological (derived from living organisms):*

Bt – *Bacillus thuringiensis* is a naturally occurring bacterium that has been safely used by organic growers for many years to control various caterpillars and foliar feeding worms. It is exceptionally safe for humans and the environment when sprayed on targeted plants only. It won't harm beneficials, bees or soil life. There are other strains of these bacteria that eradicate different pests (including beetles, fungus gnats and mosquito larvae) – so be sure to choose a variety that is suitable to your targeted insect.

Diatomaceous earth – Made from the crushed exoskeletons of microscopic sea creatures, this powder controls slugs, ants, roaches, ticks and fleas. It works by lacerating the soft bodies of these pests with its extremely sharp edges. The bug promptly dehydrates and dies. It's very safe, but it can be an irritant if inhaled and you'll have to reapply after rain.

Milky spore – Goodbye toxic lawn chemicals! Milky spore is made from a naturally occurring bacterium that attacks only the larval stage of Japanese beetles – those white, C-shaped grubs feeding on your grass roots. An extra bonus: a single application works for 10 to 15 years. Because the product takes a bit of time to thoroughly spread in the soil, optimum control is gained after the second season. An amazing alternative; safe for kids and pets (and earthworms!).

Spinosad – With low toxicity to beneficials, *Saccharopolyspora spinosa* is a great biological insecticide. It offers excellent management of potato beetles, fire ants, loopers, leafminers, caterpillars and many others. Perfect for the veggie patch.

C. *Oils, soaps and others:*

Horticultural oil – These lightweight, ultra-refined oils work by suffocating soft bodied insects like aphids, mealybugs and some scales. They are perfect for use in the orchard where a late winter application will kill any over-wintering insects or eggs. Some formulations of horticultural oil also work as a fungicide, controlling powdery mildew and botrytis. Their only downsides: they must come in direct contact with the pest to be effective and you have to take care to spray all surfaces of the plant's foliage.

Insecticidal soap – The old standby. We know why it's been around so long – it works! These soaps are made from fatty acids that dehydrate and suffocate pests. They control aphids, mites, leafhoppers, earwigs, mealybugs, grasshoppers and others. The soap must come in direct contact with the pest and it's essential that you coat the undersides of the leaves as well as the tops.

Iron phosphate – Hooray! Finally a safe alternative to conventional slug and snail baits – it's unfortunate that so many cats and dogs had to lose their lives before we got smart. Iron phosphate baits are highly successful and easy to use. Slugs stop feeding as soon as the bait is consumed, and die within a few days.

Kaolin clay – Surrounds plants and fruits with a protective layer of white, powdery clay. It deters pests who don't like landing on the film and prevents sunburn on fruits as well. Useful against codling moths in the orchard and flea beetles on eggplants.

2. Fungicides and other disease suppressors

A. *Elemental (derived from natural compounds):*

Lime sulfur – An old-fashioned remedy for all types of fungal diseases and bacterial pathogens including brown rot, scab, blight, peach leaf curl, powdery mildew, anthracnose, rust and black spot. This liquid formulation is very safe and highly effective. Lime sulfur should be on every organic gardener's shelf. The only trouble: it doesn't have a long shelf life, so only buy enough for a single season.

Copper – Use caution when using this broad-based fungicide because it can be harmful to aquatic life and some plants if used incorrectly. Use only when other techniques have not worked and be sure to mix at the appropriate rates. You can harm the soil if over-applied. Controls leaf curl, leaf spot, anthracnose, rust, fire blight, bacterial blights and others.

Potassium bicarbonate – A simple, safe solution for all fungal issues; works on contact, so the organism must be present for control. Commercial formulas of this "baking soda" product work on fruits, veggies, turf grass, ornamentals and roses. You can also make your own fungicide by combining 2 Tbsp. baking soda and 1 Tbsp. horticultural oil with a gallon of water. Apply to all leaf surfaces about every 14 to 21 days.

B. *Biologicals (derived from living organisms):*

Bacillus subtilis and *Bacillus pumilus* – Biological pathogen controls that are formulated from living bacteria, these particular species are best used as a preventive measure by beginning to apply before the problem begins. Non-toxic to beneficials, bees, mammals and other non-target critters. They combat downy and powdery mildews, rusts, bacterial spot, blight, botrytis and other mildews on veggies, fruits, ornamentals, trees and shrubs. Perfect for the organic gardener's arsenal.

C. *Botanicals (derived from plant sources):*

Botanical essential oils – May include jojoba oil, citric acid, lavender extract, mint oil and soybean oil to name just a few. Many different formulations exist, so experiment with them and find which one works best for you. They control diseases like mildews and rusts.

Compost – Yep, that's right folks…there is yet another reason to have a compost pile! Recent studies have proven that good quality compost applied as mulch to the soil's surface helps suppress numerous soil-borne pathogens including blights and mildews. And, to top it off, compost tea prevents and attacks many foliar diseases (learn more in Chapter 2's Quick Tips and Chapter 8's Advanced Quick Tips sections).

D. *Herbicides*

Clove oil – Thank goodness there are now successful alternatives to nasty chemical herbicides! Many of them are based on clove oil with additions of citric or acetic acid. These herbicides are non-selective, meaning they will kill any foliage they contact and, with perennial weeds, a repeat application may be necessary. Jess uses a clove oil-based herbicide at her farm to control plantain, dandelion, morning glory, chickweed, thistles and lots more. These are great products.

Vinegar – Many old-time growers use straight vinegar to combat weeds. It does the job, but it can alter the soil pH if used extensively. For cracks in sidewalks or areas under fences it works great.

Corn gluten meal – Another exciting discovery for organic gardeners – a non-hazardous pre-emergent herbicide. The by-product of the processing of corn, this granular formula is sprinkled onto the soil's surface. It works by not allowing a germinating seed to develop its root system. Over 90% effective in its second year of proper use (imagine…90% fewer weeds to pull!). Corn gluten meal is perfect for weed control in the lawn and perennial border. It is also a quality nitrogen source for your plants and doesn't have the harmful human and environmental side effects of a typical weed-n-feed.

Flame thrower – You may laugh, but we are completely serious! "Flamers" are great for torching those pernicious weeds. They use ignited propane to heat the plant tissue to temperatures high enough to blow out cell walls. They come in both backpack and hand held styles and work great between rows in the veggie garden, along with vineyards and driveway cracks. It's an excellent non-toxic control that works equally as well as synthetic chemicals.

There are, of course, plenty of other commercial organic products on the market, with many more being released every day. The best advice we can offer is to find what works for you.

We hope we have succeeded in arming you with the know-how and confidence to manage any pest issues that should crop up in your newly organic garden. Using this 6-step approach enables you to administer to your problems with knowledge and self-confidence. You are now part of the cure.

Weeds 101 – the word on control

Don't set yourself up for disappointment by expecting a weed-free garden. Organic or not, it's unrealistic to set your goals so high. Weeds exist, they will always exist. Long after humans are gone, there will be weeds...and cockroaches (there's a happy thought for you!).

I like to remind everyone that a weed is just a misplaced wildflower. It's simply something that is growing where we don't necessarily want it; that quality alone makes it a weed. The problem is that many weeds also have a long list of other undesirable qualities (besides cropping up where they aren't welcome). Some spread viciously, crowding out a prized groundcover; seed prolifically, making so many babies you want to pull out your hair right along with them; induce allergic reactions, a la poison ivy and ragweed; have sharp spines or thorns, think thistle and multi-flora rose; or they are just plain unattractive. Let's face it, whatever the reason, some weeds must be controlled.

Control, however, shouldn't mean complete elimination. Many weeds truly are native wildflowers and should be appreciated as a potential nectar source for beneficial insects and a food source for the larval stage of many common butterflies. If possible, tolerate a few weeds in your yard and garden for the greater good. What you absolutely can't tolerate, do your best to manage.

For good reason, you have probably been told time and again to attack weeds early in the season when they are most vulnerable, and usually smaller. Stirrup, swan-neck or circle hoes are great for taking the feet right out from under young weed seedlings, but using them on established perennial weeds will only temporarily set them back; soon enough, the roots will send out new growth. For the big guys, complete removal of the root system is your best eradication bet: relatively easy for the likes of purslane, plantain and henbit; not so easy for deep rooted weeds like dock and pokeweed or fibrous ones like chickweed and spurge.

Patience is a virtue when it comes to hand weeding and many gardeners find it therapeutic; but for gardeners who find no peace in hand weeding, other options exist:

Preventive measures – Seasonal mulching will greatly reduce the number of weeds breaking the soil surface. Be sure the mulch itself is weed-free and from a reputable source. The chart in Chapter 3 describes some of our favorite mulches and the best ways to use them. Don't pile mulch on existing perennial weeds as they will push right on through; you can, however, suffocate some newly emerged annual seedlings with a good layer of mulch early in the season, but don't consider it a sure bet.

Corn gluten meal, an organic pre-emergent herbicide can be applied early in the season to prevent new weeds from germinating. We talk a lot about this product throughout the book.

Never, ever, allow a weed to go to seed...unless of course you want a thousand weeds where you once had only one. Even if you never pull the whole weed out, cut off the flower stalk before the seeds mature and scatter. For large areas of weeds, mow weekly to prevent even small weeds from setting seeds.

Don't disturb or till areas containing weed varieties known for their extensive root systems. For weeds like Canadian thistle, field bind weed and quack grass, tilling chops the roots into many little pieces – each of which will be more than happy to make a whole new baby plant.

If you can't prevent the weeds (because you already have them) – Weed early, weed often. I always think it's better to begin regular weeding in the spring when the soil is soft and to continue to do so on a weekly basis. Depending on the size of your property, schedule weeding time on a consistent day and for a set amount of time – say 2 hours per week every Wednesday. This will prevent the weeds from getting out of control, saving you extra work in the long run and preventing a lot of headaches.

Eliminate established perennial weeds by constantly removing their shoot system. Accomplished with either weed whacking, mowing or hand removal, cut any green off as soon as you see it coming through the soil. Doing this on a consistent basis will eventually exhaust the weed and "starve" it to death.

If you go on vacation, pay a neighbor or a gardening service to weed for you. Even one or two missed weeks of weeding can have a huge effect on a gardener's morale, and on the weed population. Who needs to come home to a garden full of hairy bittercress and nutsedge?

Solarization – If you are planning to build a new garden and are starting with a lot of weeds, try solarization. Here's how it's done: till the area and rake out any dislodged weed clumps or other debris to make it smooth. Water thoroughly, then spread clear plastic polyethylene sheeting over the area, burying the edges as you go (two layers work even better than one – separate the layers with empty soft drink cans). The temperatures will get very hot under the plastic and any existing weeds and weed seeds in the top few inches will be killed (as will any soil-borne pathogens). Solarization is best done for 6-8 weeks during the warmest part of the season. Once the sheeting is removed, disturb the soil as little as possible when planting. Tilling the area will bring new, viable weed seeds up to the surface, so plant the area, then promptly cover it with mulch.

Under the Herbicide section above we gave information about using a flame thrower to control weeds. Not only do these things work great, they are very satisfying to use!

As a last resort, try the organic herbicides we discussed earlier in the chapter. And you'll want to check out the Quick Tips section for more specific weed control options.

Jess

Doug Tells All | *about excess cucumbers*

I don't think there are many pests more hated than the cucumber beetle. This green spotted or striped bug feeds on most of the cucurbit family. Though the chewing damage is minimal, the dreaded bacterial wilt that the beetles carry will destroy the plants.

For years I would plant cucumbers as soon as the danger of frost had passed, and each season I would find the beetles munching away at the leaves and lingering in the yellow blossoms. Then one day, soon after the infestation, the bacterial wilt would come; the plants would wilt and no amount of water could revive them.

During my early days of organic conversion I was perplexed with the problem. I hated to have my "normal" gardening friends seeing me fail. "All you've got to do is dust them," they would say. But that wasn't going to be the answer for me ever again. I'm one of those gardeners who doesn't want to spray anything on their crops, organic or not. So I cracked the books and found lots of ways to beat the beetle at its own game.

The first thing I did was plant my cucumbers a little later, off the life-cycle of the pest. I planted some all-female varieties under floating row covers. Since they don't need pollination to set fruit, they can grow all season under protection; and the beetles can't land on the vines. I planted a second crop in early summer and grew them up a trellis. This kept the plants off the ground and the beetles off.

The only problem I have now is, what to do with all those cucumbers? They are great gifts in the office for non-gardeners. And when I'm harvesting 10 or more a day, I'm tempted to wait at the stop sign at the bottom of the hill for an unsuspecting car with open windows. I like to imagine the driver's surprise, arriving home and seeing the back seat filled with cucumbers. I call that Christmas in July.

Jess Tells All — *about a beech*

A few years back, clients of mine had a beautiful young copper beech tree growing next to their perennial border. When the tree's upper branches began to be defoliated, the homeowner asked me to investigate. I found the culprit: tussock moth caterpillars. Knowing that the common biological control Bt would eliminate the problem, I made a single application.

Educating people about organic gardening also means teaching them patience. Bt stops the caterpillars from feeding immediately, but they don't actually die and fall off the plant until some time later. I explained this to the homeowners, assuring them that no more damage would be done to the tree.

Two days later, the landscaper came to mow the lawn and noticed the defoliation on the beech tree. He decided to take matters into his own hands and sprayed the tree with a very strong synthetic product. The day was over 90 degrees and the sun was out full force. Within a few days after the synthetic application the tree was completely defoliated; not a leaf remained. I asked the homeowners what happened, and after questioning the landscaper we had our answer. To top off the story, the landscaper then decided the tree was dead and cut it down, all the way to the ground!

*Plants are resilient. They can handle a lot of damage, both from nature and man. You not only have to be patient with the remedy, but be patient with the plant. Let it have a season or two to rebound...**before** you break out the chainsaw.*

QUICK TIPS

✄ MORE PHYSICAL AND MECHANICAL CONTROLS ✄

Cucumber beetle

Both spotted and striped cucumber beetles can be trapped on sticky, yellow cards baited with a pheromone lure. The cards, with the attached lures, are hung just above the tops of cucumber plants.

Floating row covers

This lightweight, white fabric is made to float on top of plants and provide a barrier from feeding or breeding insects. It is very useful in the veggie patch and deters cabbage looper, flea beetles, squash vine borers, carrot maggots, squash bugs, berry-eating birds, aphids, grasshoppers, leaf hoppers, and others. For crops where pollination is necessary, be sure to remove the fabric when the flowers open. Heavier weight fabrics can also be used as frost protection.

Apple maggots

For folks who grow apples, the worms that tunnel to the core are an unpleasant surprise. Hang red Christmas balls coated with sticky, non-drying glue in the tree. Two or three per dwarf apple tree will suffice. The adult insects are lured to the red traps and get stuck in the glue. Hang them in late May and re-coat with glue every month or two until harvest.

Cutworms

A simple way to keep cutworms from grazing on your seedlings: surround the young plants with a toilet paper tube "collar" sunk about 1/2 inch into the ground.

Deer

There are as many ideas for deterring deer as there are deer to foil them. We've had the greatest success with a motion-activated sprinkler that shoots hard bursts of water at them. You can also try putting a radio in the garden, tuned to a talk station. This is mostly effective for just a few nights before harvesting: deer always show up the night before you are ready to harvest those ripe melons! Switch methods often as they tend to get familiar with the same deterrent used over and over.

More deer

Fencing is the hands-down best method for keeping deer out of the garden. You'll need to make it at least 8 feet high though, because Bambi is a very good jumper. Doug likes to use a heavyweight black or green plastic mesh fence attached to 2x2 posts. For added protection, you can double up the fence; putting a 6-foot-high one about 4 feet inside the taller one. They can't jump across both at the same time; and they don't like to jump into enclosed spaces.

Again with the deer

If you have managed to fence the deer out, but don't want the fence to cross the driveway, install a cattle crossing. These metal structures are sunk into the ground and consist of evenly spaced bars that run across the driveway. Because of the big space between the bars the deer won't walk across it, but you can easily drive the car through.

Groundhogs

You can't fence them out because they either climb over it or burrow under it. You've got a few choices: live trap them, eradicate them, or run a single strand of electrified wire (solar powered ones are great) around the perimeter of the garden; about 5 inches from ground level works well.

Yellow sticky tape

This wide tape is coated in sticky, non-drying glue and is placed through a stand of infested plants. The yellow color is the attractant and is meant to draw leafhoppers, flea and cucumber beetles. Be warned, however, that it can also trap other flying insects – including bees and butterflies.

Japanese beetle traps

Those bags you find in your local garden center contain a pheromone that attracts male Japanese beetles. The trouble with them is that they have a huge range and can actually draw beetles from near and far, all of whom stop for lunch before they fly into the bag. If you are going to use them, put them very, very far from the garden – like the next acre over.

Of slugs and salt

Jess used to sprinkle salt on the slugs she'd encounter every morning in her clients' gardens; at least until the day she witnessed a slug shed its slimy coating and slither away unscathed. In our opinions, this is not a useful remedy.

Mason jar

Keep a canning jar with lid in the garden shed. Use it to collect your hand-picked pests. When you are ready to "dispose" of them, just put a cotton ball soaked with rubbing alcohol in it and close the lid. This seems somehow nicer than drowning them in soapy water...unless of course, you like to watch them squirm.

Earwigs in cardboard

If you have earwig troubles in the garden, place a few pieces of corrugated cardboard around the infested plants. They like to shelter in the "tunnels" between layers. Each morning shake the cardboard into a plastic bag to chase out the hiding insects, then put the cardboard back in the garden.

Bulbs with gravel

Gophers, chipmunks and mice love to eat bulbs. When you plant them each fall, put a few handfuls of sharp gravel or crushed oyster shells in the hole first, then put in the bulbs. Top with a few more handfuls of gravel before covering over with soil. The pointed edges will keep the critters from digging through to the bulbs.

Slugs and copper

Slugs "sizzle" when they come in contact with copper. There is a chemical reaction between the metal and something in the slug's slime. To keep slugs out of raised veggie beds, run a strip of copper along the top of the bed's frame or surround the base of your plants with a copper collar.

Flea beetles vs. plant bugs

An easy way to tell the difference between damage caused by flea beetles versus that caused by four-lined plant bugs: hold a leaf up to the sunlight. If light comes through the holes, flea beetles are your culprit. If the marks are merely translucent, plant bugs it is.

Four-lined plant bugs

These neon yellow or green striped insects are very difficult to see because they move so quickly. Plant bugs are one of only a few pests that feed on plants with highly fragranced foliage. They make perfect, round pock marks in the leaves of plants like oregano, Russian sage, lavender and others. The good news: their damage is purely aesthetic. Simply prune out the marred growth and allow new branches to develop.

⚶ WEEDS ⚶

Poison ivy

Here's a great way to safely remove poison ivy plants. Wearing protective clothing and gloves, dig out as much of the base of the plant as you can (be sure to wash the shovel and handle afterwards). Put a garbage bag (or two) over your hand and up your arm. Pick up the plant tops then flip the bag inside-out over it – pretend you are picking up a pile of dog poop. Seal the bag and throw it away. Wash up promptly, using one of the poison ivy washes you can now find at your local pharmacy.

Japanese knotweed

For stands of this invasive, exotic weed try a method called tarping. In early spring, before the shoots emerge, cover the patch with a heavy-duty tarp (like the kind you'd cover a boat or car with). Make sure to go a few feet from the outer edge of the stand. Bury the ends of the tarp completely, thus effectively blocking all light from reaching the knotweed. You'll have to leave it on for two or three seasons to gain complete control, but recent studies have shown this to be the best eradication method. Whatever you do, do not till or otherwise disturb the area...this will cause more plants to emerge.

Gin

If you can refrain from imbibing, plain gin makes a great natural contact herbicide.

Painting your weeds

When weeds grow so close to desirable plants that spraying anything is impossible, paint your weeds. Take a trim-sized paintbrush and a cup of organic herbicide and brush it on the weeds' foliage.

Ridding groundcover of grass

When grass has found its way into your Pachysandra, myrtle, winter creeper or other groundcovers, try this method. Let the grass blades get fairly long, but do not allow them to flower. Put on a chemical-resistant rubber glove, then a cotton glove on top of that. Soak a rag or sponge in an organic herbicide and grasp the tops of the grass with it. Run the rag and cotton glove along the length of the grass, being careful to avoid the plants underneath. This will kill the grass while leaving the groundcover unscathed.

ADVANCED QUICK TIPS

✄ MORE PRODUCTS ✄

Homemade soap

Though we don't usually recommend any homemade pesticides (mostly because you may do more harm than good), insecticidal soap is fairly infallible. Put just 3 or 4 drops of un-fragranced liquid dish detergent in a quart of water. Mix it well and use it on plants that are being moved indoors for the winter months. Use it once a month at most and only when insects are present.

OMRI certification

If you aren't sure if a particular product is safe for organic gardening, the Organic Materials Review Institute's website lists many of the approved substances for certified organic growing. If it's listed there, there is no doubt that it is safe for natural care. www.omri.org

Two are better than one

Invest in two pump sprayers, either hand held or backpack if you have a large area. Label one for use with organic herbicides and one for use with pesticides. Use permanent marker. This way you'll never accidentally get any herbicide residue on a desired plant.

Mixing it up

Don't ever mix pesticides, even natural ones.

Rotenone and Parkinson's

You may find rotenone listed as an organic pesticide in your favorite catalog. It is a botanical pesticide made from derris plants and can be effective against more challenging issues. However, it can be very irritating to the user and, more importantly, it has been linked to Parkinson's disease.

Shelf life

All pesticides, both conventional and natural, have a shelf life. Those derived from living organisms may require special storage. Pay attention to any label instructions detailing these issues.

✄ BENEFICIALS AND BUTTERFLIES ✄

Beneficials for weeds

Specialty organic grower catalogs now carry beneficial insects that attack particular species of weeds, mainly in the thistle family. These little guys bore into the stems and kill their hosts; might not be useful to the average gardener, but interesting nonetheless.

Monarchs and Bt

Much ado has been made lately about the possibility of butterfly larvae being killed when gardeners use Bt. Bt will kill any caterpillar that ingests it, so it should only be applied to those plants currently hosting pest caterpillars. Be aware that the spray may drift, so use it only on calm, windless days. Most species of butterfly larvae have very specific host plants (i.e. monarchs and milkweed); learning to identify these plants may prevent any possible misapplication.

Butterfly larvae

When you encounter a caterpillar in the garden that you aren't familiar with, be sure to identify it before taking any action. It may be the larva of any number of pollinating butterflies or moths. And be careful – some caterpillars, even beautiful ones, may have hairs that can give you a nasty sting.

✄ COMMUNICATION ✄

Signs on the road

If your yard borders a road that is regularly sprayed with herbicides, be sure to post "Do Not Spray" signs and manage the weeds yourself. The highway department is not organic and uses quite potent herbicides.

Organic garden signs

One of the nicest gifts Jess ever received is a garden sign that reads "An Organic Gardener Lives Here." Of course, her other favorite is one that says "Grow, Dammit."

We'll conclude this chapter (and the book) by thanking you for listening. Congratulate yourself on taking the most difficult step on the road to more responsible gardening: getting started. We look forward to the day when all gardeners comprehend the importance of their role as stewards of their little piece of earth. Follow the guiding principles of organic gardening to the best of your ability, and together we can create a safer place to garden – and a better place to live.

APPENDIX

Friends of the Organic Gardener
A Source List for All Things Organic

To find your local Cooperative Extension Agency go to the USDA website: www.csrees.usda.gov/extension/index.html. Or find it listed in the blue (government) pages of your local phone book – usually in the county government section. A Cooperative Extension Agency is a service run by state university agriculture departments to provide the public with information about farming and gardening.

Soil Tests

Available through your local Cooperative Extension Agency or through the independent labs listed below.

Woods End Soil Labs
RFD 1, Box 4050
Old Rome Road
Mt. Vernon, ME 04352
(207) 293-2457; or www.woodsend.org

A & L Agricultural Labs
7621 White Pine Road
Richmond, VA 23237
(804) 743-9401; or www.al-labs-west.com/agriculture.htm

Peaceful Valley Farm Supply
PO Box 2209 Clydesdale Court
Grass Valley, CA 95945
(888) 784-1722; or www.groworganic.com

Organic Product Suppliers *(see KEY in box below)*

Extremely Green Gardening Co. (781) 878-5397; or www.extremelygreen.com
Extremely Green provides a complete line of organic products. Good customer service and a handy website. **B, D, E, F, G, J, K**

Gardener's Supply Company. (888) 833-1412 or www.gardeners.com
Though they don't carry exclusively organic products, Gardener's Supply does have a nice selection of gardening paraphernalia and other items. **B, D, F, G, H, M**

Lee Valley Tools. (800) 871-8158; or www.leevalley.com
Every kind of gardening tool your heart could desire. **H**

Dirt Works. (802) 453-5373; or www.dirtworks.net
The perfect place to find everything you'll need to grow an organic lawn, including fertilizers, grass seed and pest controls. **B, D, E, K, L**

Grow Stuff Plus. (866) 776-9951; or www.growstuffplus.com
All kinds of stuff for growing organically. They are the only company we know of with such a huge selection of Bonsai gear. **B, D, G**

Planet Natural. (800) 289-6656; or www.planetnatural.com
Great selection of organic pest controls, lawn care products and beneficial insects. They have an excellent and easy to use website. **B, D, E, G, I, L**

Baker Creek Heirloom Seeds. (417) 924-8917; or www.rareseeds.com
If you like unusual varieties, Baker Creek is your kind of place. You'll find vegetables in this catalog you didn't even know existed: winged beans, tiger-striped melons and orange eggplants. **A**

Bobba-Mike's Garlic Farm. www.garlicfarm.com
Doug swears by Bobba-Mike's garlic – the only kind he'll grow. **C**

High Mowing Seeds. (802) 888-1800; or www.highmowingseeds.com
Jess's favorite source for organic seed. Tremendous variety, personal service, high quality, and family owned....what could be better? **A, J**

Peaceful Valley Farm Supply. (888) 784-1722; or www.groworganic.com
Peaceful Valley's got it all! Everything from soil tests to tools, equipment, seeds and pest control. Their catalog has a wealth of information; filled with charts and helpful hints. A leader in the field. **A, B, C, D, E, F, G, H, I, J, K, L, M, N**

Territorial Seed Company. (800) 626-0866; or www.territorialseed.com
Jess is fond of this company because they produce a fall catalog that gives tons of information on planting for late season harvests. Copious selection to boot. **A, D, G, H, M**

Abundant Life Seeds. (541) 767-9606; or www.abundantlifeseeds.com
Rare and extraordinary seeds found here. They also have a wonderful selection of herb and flower seeds. **A**

Johnny's Selected Seeds. (207) 861-3901; or www.johnnyseeds.com
Johnny's carries both conventional and organic seeds. Handsome selection and always a favorite for quality. **A, C, G, H**

Seeds of Change. (888) 762-7333; or www.seedsofchange.com
A seed company that specializes in preserving traditional and heirloom varieties. A little more expensive, but worth every penny. **A, J**

Fedco Seeds. No phone orders; fax (207) 873-7333; or www.fedcoseeds.com
Fedco doesn't have a fancy catalog, but they do provide great quality seeds; with a heck of a selection of both organic and conventional. They also sell fruit trees. **A, J, N**

Ronningers Potato Farm. (208) 267-3265; or www.ronningers.com
An amazing selection of potatoes from around the world, along with beautiful and unique garlic. **C, J**

Gardens Alive. (513) 354-1483; or www.gardensalive.com
One-stop organic shopping at Gardens Alive. Their catalog boasts great pictures of pests and even a program for organic fruit tree care. Plus, they often have great promotions. **B, D, E, F, G, I, K, L, M**

Ohio Earth Foods. (330) 877-9356; or www.ohioearthfood.com
This company has the best quality organic fertilizer we have ever found. Re-Vita Compost Plus is a pelletized formula both of us use religiously in our veggie gardens. Their organic potting soil is awesome too. **B, D, G**

Buglogical Control Systems. (520) 298-4400; or www.buglogical.com
Buglogical has every kind of beneficial insect you could want. **I**

Cockadoodle Doo. (877) USE-ORGANIC (873-6742); or www.purebarnyard.com
They have a four-step organic lawn care program that is second to none.
Use it: your lawn (and your spouse) will thank you. **B, D, E**

St. Gabriel Laboratories. (800) 801-0061; or www.milkyspore.com
St. Gabriel's carries milky spore grub killer along with organic fertilizers and
more. They even have an organic poison ivy control. **B, D, E, F**

Heirloom Seeds. (412) 384-0852; or www.heirloomseeds.com
This Pittsburgh-based company is a favorite for rare and unusual heirloom
seeds. They sell no hybrids and specialize in veggies with superior taste. **A**

March Biological. (800) 328-9140; or www.marchbiological.com
A must for those seeking beneficial insects and other biological controls.
They also sell everything you'll need to make compost using worms. **I**

Arbico Organics. (800) 827-2847; or www.arbico-organics.com
Organic fly control, pet care, pest control, fertilizers and lots, lots more.
If you need it, they'll have it. **B, D, E, F, H, I, L**

Burpee. (800) 888-1447; or www.burpee.com
Burpee carries several varieties of organic vegetable and herb seeds in
addition to garden tools and other growing gear. **A, B, H**

Raintree Nursery. (360) 496-6400; or www.raintreenursery.com
Jess's favorite source for bare root fruit trees. Great selection, descriptive
catalog and friendly customer service. **B, G, H, M, N**

One Green World. (877) 353-4028; or www.onegreenworld.com
Fruit and nut trees and shrubs, rootstocks and berries. Plus all the supplies
you'll need to take care of them. **B, G, N**

KEY

A	Seeds
B	Natural Pest Controls
C	Specialty Plants and Bulbs
D	Fertilizers and Soil Amendments
E	Lawn Care Products
F	Weed Control Products
G	General Garden Products (including trellisses, row covers, traps, lures and other physical insect controls)
H	Tools
I	Beneficial Insects
J	Cover Crop Seed
K	Grass Seed
L	Organic Pet Care
M	Fencing
N	Fruits, Nuts and Berries

These companies have not paid to be on this list. They are here because we have personal experience with them and think their products and service will be of benefit to you. Some of the companies carry both organic and conventional products. If you aren't sure if a product is safe for organic use, call the company and ask.

Books that you may find interesting:

The Botany of Desire: A Plant's-Eye View of the World
— by Michael Pollan

Fast Food Nation: The Dark Side of the All-American Meal
— by Eric Schlosser

This Organic Life: Confessions of a Suburban Homesteader
— by Joan Dye Gussow

The Fate of Family Farming: Variations on an American Idea
— by Ronald Jager

*Forever Green: The History and Hope of the American Fores*t
— by Chuck Leavell and Mary Welch

Pesticide Information

Toxics Information Project. (401) 351-9193; or www.toxicsinfo.org

National Coalition Against the Misuse of Pesticides. (202) 543-5450;
    or www.beyondpesticides.org

The National Resources Defense Council. (212) 727-2700; or www.nrdc.org

To Learn More About Us or to Schedule a Lecture:

Please visit our website: www.theorganicgardeners.com

Local Pittsburgh sources for organic materials:

Commercial compost

Agrecycle Inc.
(Available through many local nurseries)
For bulk purchases contact them at:
335 N Braddock Ave
Pittsburgh, PA 15208
Phone: (412) 242-7645

Nurseries and Garden Centers

Hahn Nursery
5443 Babcock Blvd.
Pittsburgh, PA 15237
Phone: (412) 635-7475

Reilly's Summer Seat Farm
and Garden Center
1120 Roosevelt Road
Pittsburgh, PA 15237
Phone: (412) 364-8270
www.ReillysSummerSeatFarm.com

Soergel's Orchard
2573 Brandt School Rd
Wexford, PA 15090
Phone: (724) 935-1743
www.soergels.com

Gardenalia
252 S Highland Ave
Pittsburgh, PA 15206
Phone: (412) 441-9611

Construction Junction
North Lexington and Mead Streets
Pittsburgh, PA 15206
Phone: (412) 243-5025

Janoski's Greenhouse
1714 State Route 30
Clinton, PA 15026
Phone: (724) 899-3438
www.janoskis.com

LMS Nursery
3312 A Wagner Road
Allison Park, PA 15101
Phone: (412) 767-7020

Seeds

Heirloom Seeds
PO Box 245
West Elizabeth, PA 15088
Phone: (412) 384-0852
www.heirloomseeds.com

Trax Farms
528 Trax Road
Finleyville, PA 15332
Phone: (412) 835-3246
www.traxfarms.com

Best Feeds
2105 Babcock Blvd.
Pittsburgh, PA 15209
Phone: (412) 822-7777

Bakerstown Feed
5820 Rte 8
Bakerstown, PA 15007
Phone: (724) 443-7600

Sestili Nursery
3721 Swinburne St.
Pittsburgh, PA 15213
Phone: (412) 681-1200

The Urban Gardener
1901 Brighton Road
Pittsburgh, PA 15212
Phone: (412) 323-GROW

Chapon's Greenhouse and Supply
4846 Streets Run Road
Pittsburgh, PA 15236
Phone: (412) 881-1520

Garden Dreams Urban Farm and Nursery
404 Center Street
Pittsburgh, PA 15221
Phone: (412) 638-3333

GLOSSARY

Acidic – anything having a pH less than 7 as a result of containing excess hydrogen molecules

Aerating – removing cores of soil in turf to reduce compaction and introduce air to the root zone

Aggregates – a mixture of soil components gathered together into a clump

Alkaline – anything having a pH more than 7 as a result of containing excess hydroxide molecules

Annual – any plant whose life cycle is completed in one year; may also be used to reference a plant that does not survive the winter

Aphid mummy – the outer shell remaining after a predator has consumed the fleshy inside of an aphid

Bacterial wilt – a disease caused by many species of bacteria that causes a plant to wilt and die rapidly; usually spread by insects

Beneficial insect – a predatory or parasitic insect that feeds on common garden pests

Biological controls – any pest control derived from a living organism including bacteria, nematodes, fungus and beneficial insects

Bio-solids – human sewage sludge

Blight – the response to an attack by a bacteria, fungus or mold; it typically begins with leaf spots and lesions then progresses to yellowing and death of various plant parts

Border fork – a short handled, flat bladed pitchfork, usually with four tines

Botanical – derived from plant sources

Cation exchange capacity (CEC) – an indicator of soil fertility that describes the soil's ability to hold onto positively charged minerals

Chlorosis – the yellowing of leaves as a result of disease or nutrient deficiency

Cistern – a tank for catching and storing rainwater; usually underground

Clay – the smallest mineral particle in a soil sample; it is flat and very sticky

Cloche – a bell-shaped cover placed over a plant to protect it and speed its growth

Companion planting – planting two or more different plants in close proximity to each other for their mutual benefit

Compost – a mixture of decaying organic substances used for amending soil; ingredients can include leaves, grass clippings, plant trimmings, manures, kitchen scraps (no meats, bones or dairy) and other garden debris

Compost tea – a liquid made from compost steeped in water; used as a fertilizer and disease suppressant

Conifer – an evergreen plant that bears cones

Corn gluten meal – a product used as a pre-emergent herbicide derived from the processing of corn; also used as a nitrogen fertilizer

Cover crop – a crop planted to prevent soil from eroding and to add nutrients to the soil after decomposition

Cross-pollination – the transfer of pollen from one plant to another

Crown division – propagating a plant by dividing its crown

Cultural practices – any technique or method that involves manipulating a plant and/or its surroundings; including pruning, fertilizing, staking, trellising, deadheading and other general procedures

Cuttings – portions of plants used for vegetative propagation. Can be roots, stems or leaves

Deadheading – the removal of spent flowers

Dolomitic limestone – a type of agricultural lime that contains both calcium and magnesium; generally used to raise soil pH

Drip system – a method of irrigation that uses perforated hoses at ground level to slowly seep water into a plant's root zone

Elemental sulfur – a kind of granular fertilizer made of sulfur used to lower soil pH

Endophyte enhanced – grass seed that is infected with a beneficial fungus that helps it fight off diseases and insects

Espalier – a technique of pruning and training a tree to grow flat or two-dimensional

Exoskeleton – the external covering of an insect

Fertilizer – any substance used to add nutrients to the soil

Fescue – several varieties of grass, many of which are suited to shady conditions

Fish emulsion – an organic liquid fertilizer made from fish by-products

Floating row cover – a translucent spun-bound fabric that is used to shield crops from temperature extremes and pests

Frost dates – the average date of either the first or last frost for any given hardiness zone

Fungicide – a substance used for destroying fungus

Fungus – organisms that feed on the decomposition of organic materials; including molds, mushrooms, rusts, yeasts, smuts and mildews.

Grafting – a method of propagation where the tissues from one plant are united with tissues from another, allowing the two plants grow as one.

Green manure – a cover crop

Hand lens – a small magnifying glass

Hardiness zone – a geographic area defined by the maximum and minimum temperatures; usually a plant will be referred to as being hardy to a particular zone

Heirloom – an old-fashioned, open-pollinated variety of plant usually introduced more than 50 years ago; a non-hybrid plant

Herbicide – a substance used for destroying plants

Honeydew – the sweet, stick excrement of any number of soft bodied insects, including aphids, scales and mealy bugs

Humus – any organic matter that has reached the point of decomposition where it is stable and can break down no further

Hybrid – the offspring of two different varieties of plants; usually created to combine the positive attributes of both parents into one plant

Insecticide – a substance used for destroying insects

Landscape fabric – a black, perforated fabric used on the soil surface to block weed growth and warm soil

Larvae – an early life stage of any insect that undergoes a metamorphosis

Leaf mold or leaf humus – compost derived from decomposed leaves

Legume – any member of the pea and bean family of plants; all legumes have the ability to convert nitrogen from the air into a form that other plants can use

Lime – a calcium-based compound derived from limestone that is used to raise soil pH

Living mulch – a crop planted to suppress weeds, stabilize soil temperatures and reduce watering; usually planted under and around taller plants

Microbes – a minute life form or microorganism; may refer to any number of bacteria species

Monoculture – growing only one type of crop or plant in an area

Mulch – any substance applied to the soil's surface to reduce watering, stabilize soil temperatures and suppress weeds

Mulching mower – a lawn mower designed to chop the grass clippings into small particles and redistribute them onto the soil surface

Mushroom soil or mushroom compost – a special compost initially used to grow mushrooms and then used as an organic matter source for gardens; usually consisting of decomposed corn cobs, wheat straw, hay, manures and other ingredients

Mycorrhiza – a fungus that forms a symbiotic relationship with a plant by penetrating the roots and providing certain nutrients to the plant in exchange for carbohydrates the plant manufactures during photosynthesis; 95% of plant species have a partnership with mycorrhiza

Nematode – a microscopic roundworm; some species are beneficial and prey on pests like cutworms and borers, while other species are pests, attacking roots and causing distorted growth

Nitrogen fixing – the process of converting nitrogen in the air into a form that is usable by plants

Nutrient – an element or compound necessary for plant growth

Open-pollinated – a variety resulting from natural pollination by wind or insects as opposed to human pollination (which is a hybrid)

Organic matter – any material that is the product of the decomposition of once-living organisms

Ornamental – any annual, perennial, tree or shrub planted to provide beauty

Pathogen – a bacteria or fungus that causes disease or decline

Perennial – an herbaceous plant whose life cycle takes two or more years to complete; a plant that survives winter temperatures but is not considered a woody shrub or tree

Pesticide –a substance used for destroying any pest; includes insects, plants, mites and fungus

pH – the measure of acidity or alkalinity of something; the amount of hydrogen and hydroxide molecules present

Pheromone trap – a trap that is baited with a synthetic version of a compound that insects release to attract a mate

Potting mix – a mixture of peat moss, vermiculite, perlite and/or other ingredients that is used for growing in containers

Predator – a creature that exists by preying on and consuming other organisms

Pre-emergent herbicide – an herbicide that works by preventing seed from germinating or by preventing a seedling from breaking through the soil's surface

Prey – any living organism eaten by another creature

Primary macronutrients – the three minerals used in the largest quantity during a plant's life; they are nitrogen, phosphorus, and potassium

Propagation – the creation of new plants either through sexual (seeds or spores) means or asexual (vegetative) means

Pupate – an insect passing through one life stage into another

Raised beds – garden areas that are higher than the existing ground level; areas usually built up with extra soil and organic matter that may be contained in a frame of wood, stone, block, etc.

Rooting hormone – a powder or liquid containing auxins, the class of plant hormones responsible for generating new roots and promoting cell division, applied to vegetative cuttings in hopes of promoting quick and ample root growth. Natural versions are derived from willow species that contain a high amount of auxins.

Sand – the largest mineral particle of soil; gritty and loose

Scarification – breaking the seed coat of some varieties to ease germination; can be done with pre-soaking, filing, nicking or scoring the seed coat

Silt – very fine particles of mineral fragments in soil; intermediate in size between sand and clay

Slow release fertilizer – a fertilizer whose formulation enables it to release nutrients into the soil over a long period of time

Soaker hose – a plastic or rubber hose perforated with tiny holes that slowly leach out water; usually placed at or just under the soil surface so that the water is applied only to the root zone of the plants

Soil amendment – any organic matter incorporated into the soil for the purpose of adding nutrients, increasing water holding capacity, feeding microbes and building soil structure

Soil-borne disease – any pathogen present in the soil; usually spread by infected soil splashing up onto leaves during irrigation or rain

Soil compaction – the compression of soil particles as a result of pressure on the soil's surface; will result in less room for air and water in the soil and reduced root growth

Soil solarization – a process used to kill weeds, weed seeds, and soil-borne pathogens in the top few inches of the soil; it traps heat from the sun under plastic sheeting, effectively "burning out" the pest

Soil structure – the way the mineral and organic matter particles in any soil aggregate (or clump) together; it determines how air, water and nutrients move around in the soil; and it determines to some extent how easily roots are able to penetrate the soil

Soil test – a laboratory test to determine nutrient levels, organic matter levels, pH and other qualities of a soil

Soil texture – the proportion of sand, silt and clay particles in any given soil

Stratification – seeds are treated to artificially simulate winter conditions and bring on germination

Symbiotic relationship – a relationship where both parties reap benefits

Synthetic – anything man-made, usually in a laboratory

Thatch – a thick layer of dead plant matter, including leaves, stems and roots, that builds up underneath grass plants

Tilling – turning over the soil by hand or with a mechanical rototiller

Top dress – applying organic matter to the soil surface without tilling it in

Totipotency – the ability of a plant cell to divide and produce any plant part; all the genetic information is contained within each and every cell, no matter what part of a plant it came from

Trace nutrients – elements that are essential for plant growth, but they are only used in very small quantities

Vegetative propagation – a form of asexual reproduction that creates new plants from existing plant parts instead of seeds or spores; some species of plants naturally propagate themselves by sending out specialized roots, runners or other modified plant tissues

Vermiculture – raising earthworms for their castings

Verticutter – a machine used for de-thatching the lawn

Water soluble fertilizer – a fertilizer that dissolves in water and is applied during irrigation

Weed fabric – black, perforated fabric laid on the soil surface to prevent weeds

Wood ashes – ashes from fireplaces, woodstoves and fire pits

Woody perennial – a plant whose life cycle lasts two or more years, has woody rather than fleshy stems, and has above-ground growth that survives the winter

Worm castings – worm manure

Zone – see hardiness zone

Index

ACKNOWLEDGMENTS

From both of us

Thank you to Paul Kelly of St. Lynn's Press for attending one of our lectures and "seeing" this book in us. Paul, you have been a thoughtful and caring guide through the entire process, answering endless emails and tolerating all of our creative mischief. Thanks, Paul, for taking the chance.

Catherine Dees, our editor: inspiring, balanced, fair and enthusiastic through this whole journey. Thank you, Catherine, for your guidance, structure and for doing what you do best – keeping a pair of rowdy first-time authors on track.

Special thanks go to Rob Cardillo for providing us with the gorgeous photograph on the book's cover. Always professional, always patient, always perfect...Rob, you're the best!

To Evan and Jodi Verbanic of Cherry Valley Organics: thank you for supplying us with those visually delectable flowers and veggies on the cover. They are proof that organic is beautiful.

Martha Swiss, thank you for your hospitality, the iced tea, and for accommodating our impromptu photo shoot. Both you and your garden are as lovely as they come.

Thanks also to WYEP and KDKA for giving us a home and for helping us spread the word about responsible gardening. To Rob Pratte and Steve Hansen of KDKA radio in Pittsburgh – thanks for heartily welcoming us onto the airwaves; and for making us feel right at home behind the mic.

To our Mrs. Know-it-all, Denise Schreiber: your good nature and good advice are always appreciated.

Thanks to Andy Starnes for waking up early on a Sunday to shoot the image of us for the back cover. You're a real pro.

Doug Thanks All

To my wife Cindy, sons Tim and Matt, and my daughter Stephanie: thank you for supporting me through embracing the quality time we have together (even though the quantity isn't what it should be).

To my mother Gloria who showed me the joy of growing tomato plants.

To my grandmother Janet for providing me with many memories of her wonderful garden in the Lisbon ravine.

To Jess for being my work partner, putting up with my smart-ass comments and enduring the perpetual aroma of garlic I so proudly exude.

To Ed: thanks for being my best friend since 5th grade, for enduring my relentless organic speeches and for doing the right thing – gardening without chemicals.

Jess Thanks All

Thank you, John, for your love, your patience, your spirit and your inspiration. I love you.

To my little guy Ty: your smile is the light of my life.

Thank you, Mom and Dad, for a lifetime of guidance and good advice (oh, and thanks for paying for college, too!).

Thanks to the Schneider family for hiring me all those years ago: working in your greenhouse taught me the power of plants and to appreciate what a labor of love gardening can be.

Nancy Knauss and Marjorie Radebaugh deserve a big thank you for giving me my first post-college job at The Pittsburgh Civic Garden Center; and for teaching me how to teach.

To Amy and Heather: thanks for being my best friends and for tolerating me over the years. Love you.

Thank you, Paul Wiegman, for inviting me onto the radio. My life would not be the same were it not for you.

Doug, thanks for pushing me to be my best and for encouraging me to put myself out there. Working together has been the most exciting professional experience of my life. You are a true friend.

To my Nana: thank you for your beautiful garden, for the beautiful memories and for your "green" genes.

ABOUT THE AUTHORS

Doug Oster is a garden columnist for the *Pittsburgh Post-Gazette*; his herb and cooking column is distributed nationally by the LA Times Syndicate. Doug is co-host of "The Organic Gardeners" each week on KDKA radio, and is a regular guest on two Pittsburgh television stations. He is a popular lecturer at garden clubs and conferences.

Jessica Walliser has a degree in horticulture and is co-host of "The Organic Gardeners" on KDKA radio. She is a regular contributor to many national and regional gardening publications and lectures at garden clubs and botanic gardens across the country.

Doug and Jessica can be reached on the web at:
www.theorganicgardeners.com